BON APPÉTIT

Complete Branding for Restaurants, Cafés and Bakeries

SendPoints

BON APPÉTIT
Complete Branding for Restaurants, Cafés and Bakeries

© 2018 SendPoints Publishing Co., Ltd.

EDITED & PUBLISHED BY SendPoints Publishing Co., Ltd.
PUBLISHER: Lin Gengli
PUBLISHING DIRECTOR: Lin Shijian
CHIEF EDITOR: Lin Shijian
EXECUTIVE EDITOR: Li Weiji
ART DIRECTOR: He Wanling
EXECUTIVE ART EDITOR: Peng Peng
PROOFREADING: Sundae Li, Li Weiji

REGISTERED ADDRESS: Room 15A Block 9 Tsui Chuk Garden, Wong Tai Sin, Kowloon, Hong Kong
TEL: +852-35832323 / **FAX:** +852-35832448
OFFICE ADDRESS: 7F, 9th Anning Street, Jinshazhou, Baiyun District, Guangzhou, China
TEL: +86-20-89095121 / **FAX:** +86-20-89095206
BEIJING OFFICE: Room 107, Floor 1, Xiyingfang Alley, Ande Road, Dongcheng District, Beijing, China
TEL: +86-10-84139071 / **FAX:** +86-10-84139071
SHANGHAI OFFICE: Room 307, Building 1, Hong Qiang Creative Zhabei District, Shanghai, China
TEL: +86-21-63523469 / **FAX:** +86-21-63523469

SALES MANAGER: Sissi
TEL: +86-20-81007895
EMAIL: overseas01@sendpoints.cn
WEBSITE: www.sendpoints.cn / www.spbooks.cn

ISBN 978-988-14703-4-8

All rights reserved. No part of this publication may be reproduced, stored in a retrieval system or transmitted in any form or by any means, electronic, mechanical, photocopying, recording or otherwise, without prior permission in writing from the publisher. For more information, please contact SendPoints Publishing Co., Ltd.
Printed and bound in China.
Second printing

Creating a design that pleases the palate far before diners have a glimpse at the menu is an exercise that starts by creating desires. This process goes by a deep understanding of the venue's culinary approach. Translating the chef's vision for the cuisine into our design brings a consistent and a logical development.

Maxime Dautresme

Founding Partner of Substance studio, Hong Kong

CONTENTS

RESTAURANTS

◆ Regional Cuisine ◆

010	....	The Local Mbassy
014	....	BA 53
018	....	Clérigos Vinhos & Petiscos
020	....	Set Cafè
024	....	Vora Estany
026	....	Grüner Michel
030	....	Hornhuset
032	....	Kessalao
036	....	Hay Market
040	....	Brie-Bon
044	....	Galo Kitchen
046	....	Garçon
048	....	Ristorante Firenze
050	....	La Riera
052	....	La Bottega
054	....	Clifford Pier
056	....	Barabulya
058	....	Guzman Y Gomez
060	....	Casa Virginia
062	....	El Cariñito
064	....	Gymkhana
066	....	Kricket
068	....	KHA
070	....	Le Garçon Saigon
074	....	Sassy's Red
078	....	Idol Restaurant
082	....	Tumamigui
086	....	RAW
090	....	Mikôto
092	....	Thanks on the Table
094	....	4ECK
098	....	Noodle Theater
100	....	Corner House
104	....	MIU Creative Cuisine

◆ Seafood ◆

108	....	Catch and Release
112	....	The Pelican
114	....	The Ocean
118	....	Oyster´s & Co

◆ Fast Food ◆

120	....	Simple.
126	....	Botánica

128	....	Mary Wong
132	....	Pig´s Pearls
136	....	Holly Burger
138	....	Burger Circus
142	....	Burger & Love
144	....	Burger House
146	....	Better Burger
150	....	El Pollerio
152	....	Pelman Hand Made Café
156	....	Da Pizza Project

◆ Kitchen and Bar ◆

160	....	Hotshot
164	....	La Condesa
166	....	Tamarindo
168	....	Kakhovka Bar
172	....	Sagrado
176	....	Una Kitchen & Microbrewery
178	....	Santa Monica Yacht Club
182	....	Puebla 109
186	....	En Vain
188	....	Mama Liu & Sons
190	....	Banyan Bar & Refuge

◆ Restaurant and More ◆

194	....	PLY
198	....	Graanmarkt 13
202	....	Never Ending Story

CAFÉS AND BAKERIES

◆ Café ◆

206	....	Kuglóf
208	....	Coffee House London
210	....	Cafe Decada
212	....	Le Marché Cafe
216	....	Café Frida
218	....	Papa Palheta
220	....	Coffee Maker
222	....	No. Six Depot
224	....	Sei Kee Cafe
226	....	Abarrotes Delirio
230	....	Galician Strudel

◆ Bakery ◆

232	....	The Dough Collective
234	....	Don de l'Amour
236	....	Carlotta
238	....	Maitre Choux

◆ Dessert ◆

240	....	Enjoyer
242	....	Sweet Spoon
244	....	Remicone
248	....	Cowch Dessert Bar
252	....	Casca

LOCAL MBASSY

The Local Mbassy

The Local Mbassy is a boutique café and kitchen paying homage to the locals of the 1920s, especially those who made a difference in molding up the contemporary Australian art, fashion and coffee culture. The idea was to create a destination store that can play a crucial role in Sydney's social and foodie culture while serving the perfect brew of Campos Speciality Coffee. The boiler room inspired interior comes with rigueur exposed beams and bulbs, raw concrete finishes, one off refurbished furniture and a larger-than-life feature mural that sets context and tone to 1920s Australia.

HOW MUCH WOOD COULD A WOODCHUCK CHUCK,
IF A WOODCHUCK COULD CHUCK WOOD?

A B C D E F G H I J K L M N O P Q R S
T U V W X Y Z 1 2 3 4 5 6 7 8 9 0

/

Designer: Korolos Ibrahim
Artist: Sid Tapia
Photographer: Shayben Moussa

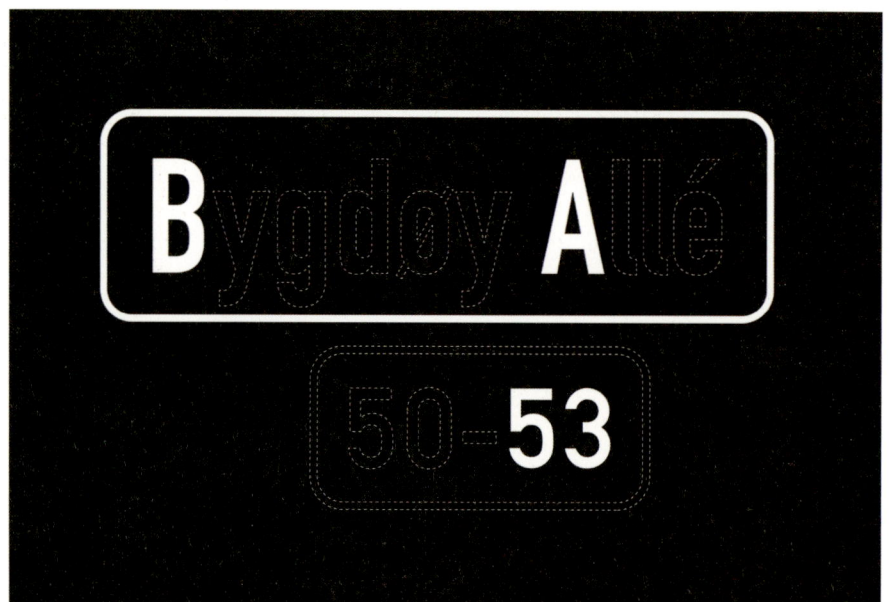

Studio: Pocket
Designer: Nicklas Lindholm Haslestad
Photographer: Marte Garmann

BA 53

The identity was inspired by the location of the restaurant, the old building Bygdøy Allé 53, and the equally iconic street signs in Oslo. It aims to reflect the brand's freshness and purity alongside tradition and history, and to merge with the celebrity chef's innovative style. The color scheme was chosen based on the fact that the menu of BA 53 changes to keep pace with the Nordic seasons.

Bygdøy Allé 53

REGIONAL CUISINE

017

Studio: White Studio
Art Director: Eduardo Aires
Designer: Ana Simões, Raquel Rei, Jorge Amador

Clérigos Vinhos & Petiscos

Clérigos serves an eclectic menu, from tapas and special wines to traditional Portuguese food and sushi. The identity was inspired by the interior design by Bastir, which combines the classic burelé pattern and traditional tiles with contemporary patterns and textures. To keep a fresh vibe, old sayings and jokes were included in the menus, which became an assortment of newspapers, flyers and placemats, shaping an interesting customer experience.

Set Cafè

Located next to Banyoles Lake, Set Cafè is a restaurant known for its use of natural local produce. This inspired the creation of a font named Patata Condensed made with potato stamps. The logo plays with the composition of letters inside a geometric shape that resembles a plate. The brand image came out to be fresh, fun and playful.

Studio: Enserio
Designer: Miquel Amela, Ferran Rodíguez

REGIONAL CUISINE

Passeig Darder, 55, 17820 Banyoles (Girona). Spain

021

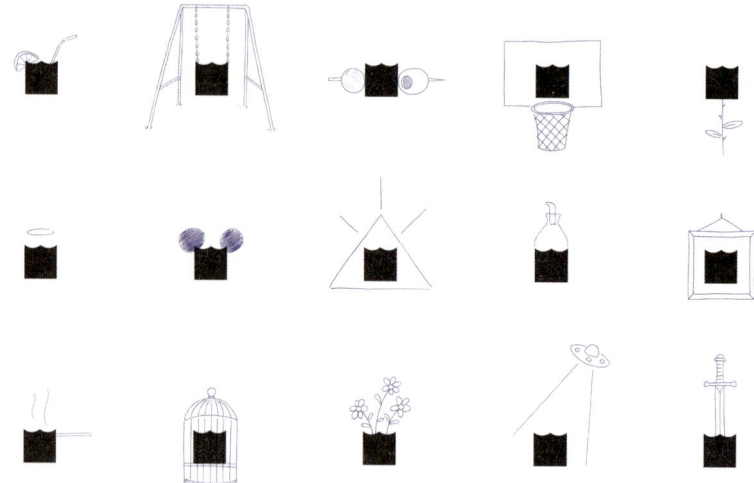

Vora Estany

The identity for the restaurant was based on a combination of a powerful abstract symbol with pen illustrations that add richness and infinite imagination to the brand image. The pen became a humorous touch to the identity to the point that even the cursor of the website is a drawing pen.

Studio: Enserio
Designer: Miquel Amela, Ferran Rodríguez

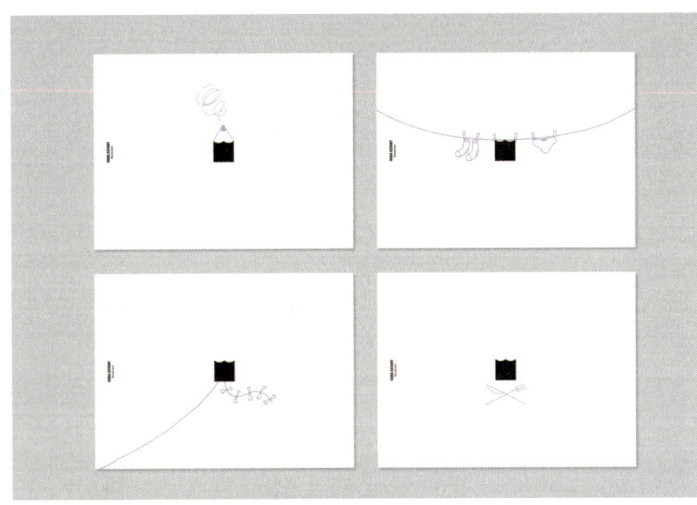

Passeig Antoni Gaudí, 3, 17820 Banyoles (Girona), Spain

Grüner Michel

With Grüner Michel, the Swabian city Leonberg in Southern Germany became home to a new gastronomic highlight. Apart from its incredibly delicious vegan dishes, the restaurant also delights your visual sense with the playful corporate design, inviting you to dine and be amazed.

Studio: ADDA STUDIO
Creative Director: Christian Vögtlin
Designer: Christian Vögtlin, Nadine März
Photographer: Melanie März

Hornhuset

Hornhuset is a bustling melting pot for those who want to enjoy a menu of small flavorful dishes. Representing a mix of all the good things from around the Mediterranean area is the core of the brand identity. Fresh bold colors, playful typography and binding frame—all conveying a sun bleaching feeling of summer.

Studio: Under
Designer: Tobias Ottomar

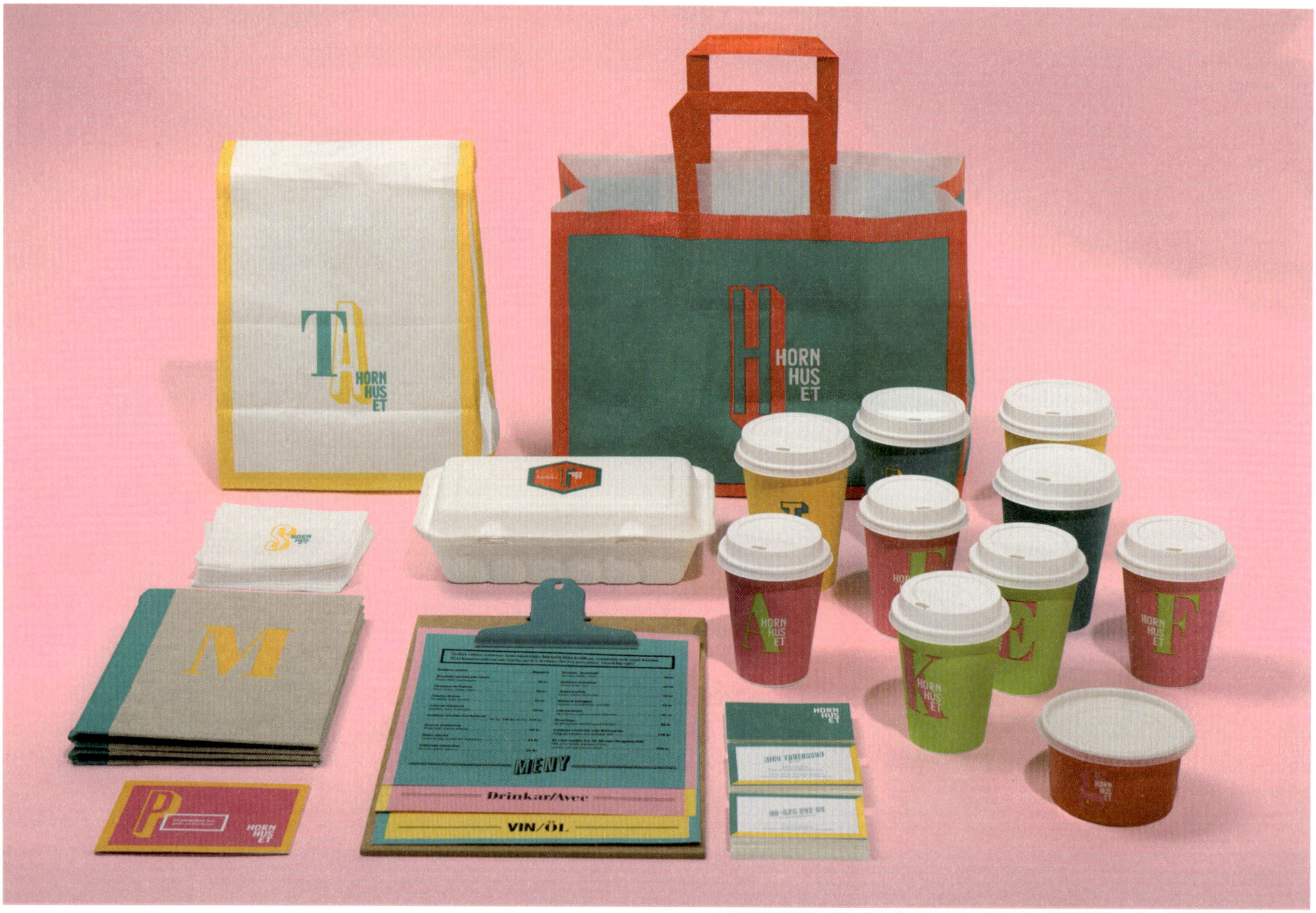

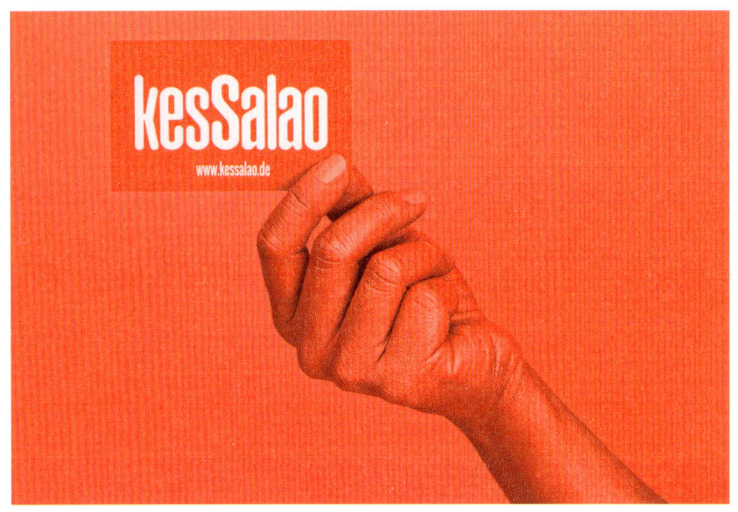

Studio: Masquespacio
Creative Director: Ana Milena Hernández Palacios
Architect junior: Virgínia Hinarejos
Graphic Designer junior: Ana Diaz
Creative junior: Carolina Micó
Photographer: David Rodríguez y Carlos Huecas

Kessalao

Kessalao is a take away restaurant specializing in Mediterranean food. The brand name combining the German "Kess" and the Spanish "Salao" is a wordplay meaning cool and amusing boy. The logo features the image of a drop of olive oil which is the essential in Mediterranean cuisine. In terms of the interior design, a range of popular colors for Germans are chosen, with red as the main color and marine blue and yellow as a reminder of the Mediterranean Sea while purple adding a strong visual touch. Birch veneer is used for the walls and pine for the furniture to create a modest and natural space.

REGIONAL CUISINE

Bonner Talweg 88 – 53113 Bonn, Germany

REGIONAL CUISINE

Hay Market

Hay Market is a restaurant set in the sprawling grounds of the Hong Kong Jockey Club. With Hong Kong Jockey Club's pedigree as a British Colonial entity, the basis of the brand concept and language is British eccentricity. Inspired by vibrant jockey silks with centuries of history, the restaurant's visual language is an eclectic mix of bold geometric shapes juxtaposed with vintage British typography and Victorian illustrations from old advertisements. The brand's logo is a playful update on classic letterforms and also functions as a blank canvas, allowing for quirky permutations when combined with different illustrations.

Studio: Foreign Policy
Creative Director: Yah-Leng Yu
Art Director: Yah-Leng Yu, Liquan Liew
Designer: Liquan Liew, Vanessa Lim, Yah-Leng Yu

REGIONAL CUISINE

2F Grandstand II, Sha Tin Racecourse, Hong Kong

Brie-Bon

Dim lights, an outdoor terrace and a decor that evokes the image of classic Parisian bistros from the 30s and 40s characterize the bistro bar Brie-Bon. The embossed ceiling and dark wood tables give an air of sobriety and elegance. The presence of plants creates a romantic atmosphere that connects visitors with the life in some parts of Paris.

Studio: PLASMA NODO

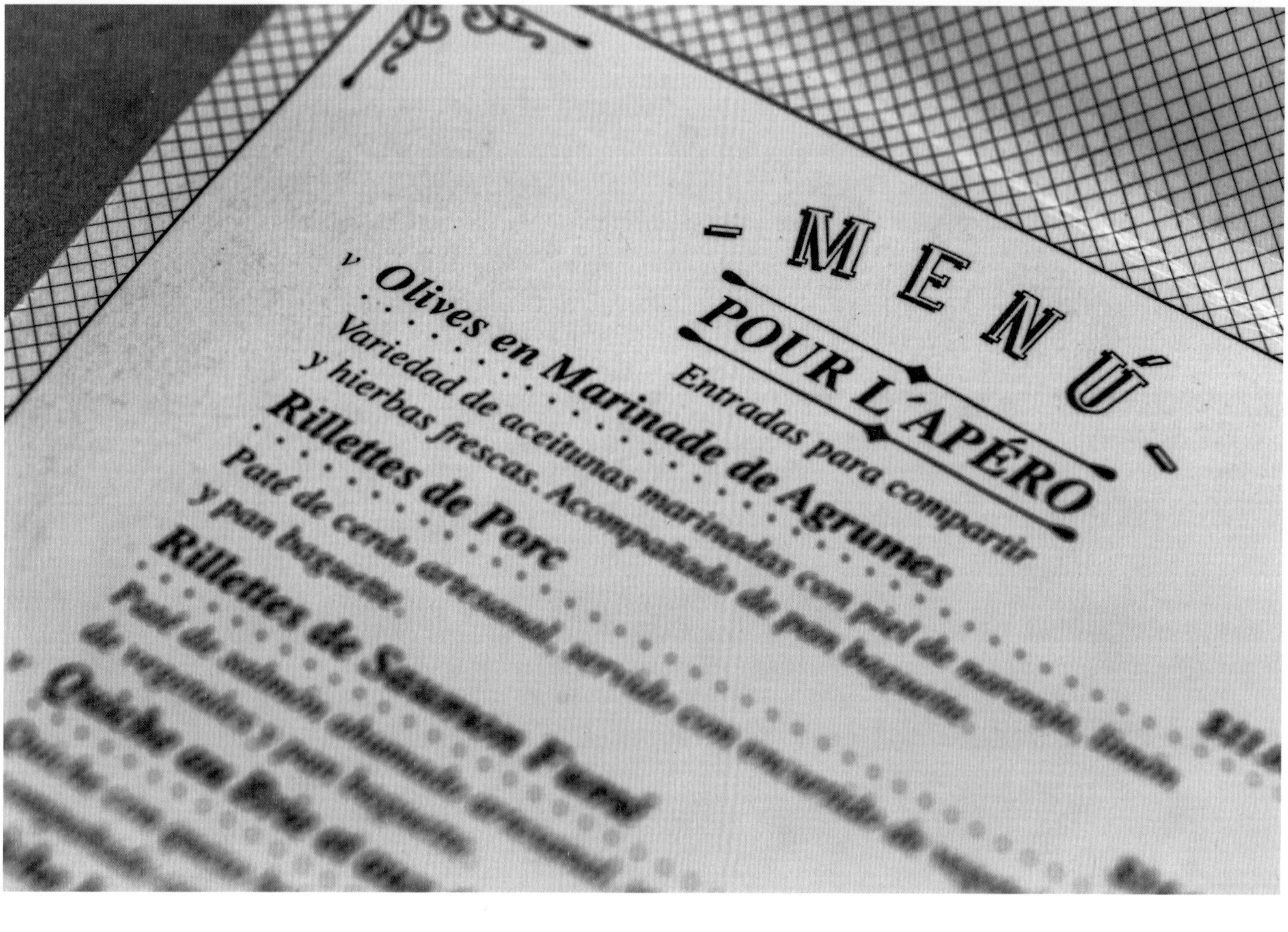

REGIONAL CUISINE

Carrera 35, no.7-118, Vía Provenza, Medellín, Colombia

041

Galo Kitchen

Galo Kitchen is a restaurant specializing in French-American cuisine. Its prime focus is breakfast, with its own in-house bakery that makes freshly baked bread and pastries. It also offers lunch and dinner menus and a cozy atmosphere all day long. The black and white skewed pattern dresses up the brand as friendly, snug and casual, a feeling supported by the logotype's organic cursive script. The zeppelin icon was inspired by the restaurant's specialty Zeppelin sandwich.

Studio: Anagrama

REGIONAL CUISINE

JRío Amazonas Oriente 333, Del Valle, 66220 San Pedro Garza García, NL, Mexico

Garçon

Garçon is a newly established French bistro, bar and patisserie that has become a favorite spot thanks to its unique offerings of good food, warm atmosphere and sociable crowd. As its name suggests, it is all about exploring the delights of youth. Based on this approach, the branding's classy Parisian theme was incorporated with modern and edgy twists in the form of geometric designs with a touch of gold.

Studio: Brownfox Studio
Designer: Fergie Tan, Amelia Agustine

REGIONAL CUISINE

Plaza Senayan Level 4 No. 410, Jakarta, Indonesia

047

Ristorante Firenze

The Firenze is a traditional Italian restaurant opened in 1974. In addition to logo redesign, the task was to create a completely new concept and design for menu and wine cards, vouchers, brochures, business cards, letterhead and website. The idea behind the identity was to lay the focus on the fresh products the restaurant is well known for and to reinterpret the classical Italian colors in a modern way.

Designer: Sarah Le Donne

REGIONAL CUISINE

Idsteiner Str. 98, 65527 Niedernhausen, Germany

049

La Riera

Opened its door in 1982, La Riera is a pizzeria that honors the traditional way of making a pizza: baking in a wood-fired oven. Though La Riera remains loyal to the traditions and purity of a transalpine kitchen, their new identity has adopted a more modern flavor, yet the authenticity of a high quality Italian restaurant remained unchanged.

Studio: Le Maritime Studio
Designer: Christelle Le Guillard
Interior Design: Núria Le Guillard

REGIONAL CUISINE

Av. Cavall Bernat 86, 17250 Platja d'Aro, Girona, Spain

La Bottega

La Bottega boasts of itself as a place that best explicates the word "original", with an informal feeling of ancient trattoria. The newly designed logo is unique with the use of formal Bodonian custom typeface. The materials used are the top-of-the-charts Fedrigoni Materica paper in rust and limestone color.

Studio: KIDSTUDIO
Designer: Marco Innocenti, Luca Parenti, Giorgio Franceschini
Photographer: Stefano Casati, Alex Teuscher

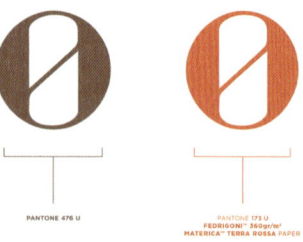   

REGIONAL CUISINE

Grand-Rue 3, Geneva, Switzerland

053

Clifford Pier

Holding onto its heritage, The Clifford Pier draws from its legacy as a bustling port in Singapore during the 1930s. Ginger flower motifs pay homage to William Farquhar who was fascinated with local botany during his time on the island. Collaterals with color palette in sea-foam, coral and Caspian blue; classic postage stamps accented with tropical flora and fauna, along with architectural elements, are reminiscent of the glorious voyages that set sail from this historical landmark.

Studio: Foreign Policy
Creative Director: Yah-Leng Yu
Art Director: Liquan Liew
Designer: Yah-Leng Yu, Liquan Liew, Adeline Tan
Illustrator: Adeline Tan

REGIONAL CUISINE

The Fullerton Bay Hotel, 80 Collyer Quay, 049326 Singapore

055

Barabulya

Barabulya is a Black Sea cuisine restaurant siatuated in the Spartak yacht club offering Georgian, Armenian, Ossetian, Odessa and Sochi cuisines. The logo and corporate identity were inspired by the atmosphere of a city restaurant popular in the Soviet Union in the 70s and 80s. The watercolor red mullet in the raster version of the logo resembles the illustration in the scientific publication of the 19th century.

Studio: Province design

REGIONAL CUISINE

Naberezhnaya St., 4A, Dolgoprudny, Moscow Region, Russia

057

Guzman Y Gomez

The characters of Guzman and Gomez, the inspiration behind the founding of the restaurant, is the focus of the identity. The white star shape in the identity creates an impression of a lemon or lime commonly used in Mexican cuisine. A system of typeface was developed from the concept of letters created out of tapeto reinforce the typical Mexican vibe.

Studio: The Creative Method
Creative Director: Tony Ibbotson

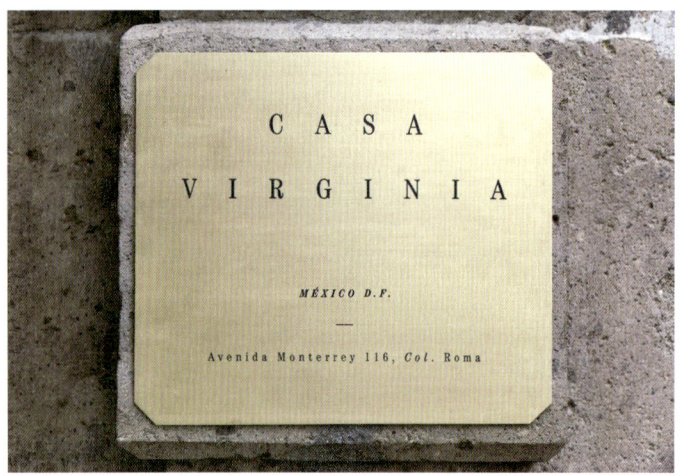

Casa Virginia

Casa Virginia is Chef Mónica Patiño's latest culinary project in Mexico City's Roma neighborhood where she looks to glorify and reenact a homely experience. The same philosophy and ideals are reflected in the graphic applications where special attention has been paid to the smallest details such as gold foiling finish, imitating the chef's meticulous process in cooking. The identity was developed as a contemporary reinterpretation of the traditional graphic language which was popular in Mexico in the 1920s.

Studio: Savvy
Interior: Habitación 116

El Cariñito

El Cariñito aims to evoke a laid-back marketplace atmosphere with hints of Mexican elements in the branding. The smells, the humble elements in a regular marketplace kitchen, the way people solve graphic issues by hand, and the particular language to express traditional ingredients, have served as inspiration and set accurately the design background.

Designer: Abraham Lule

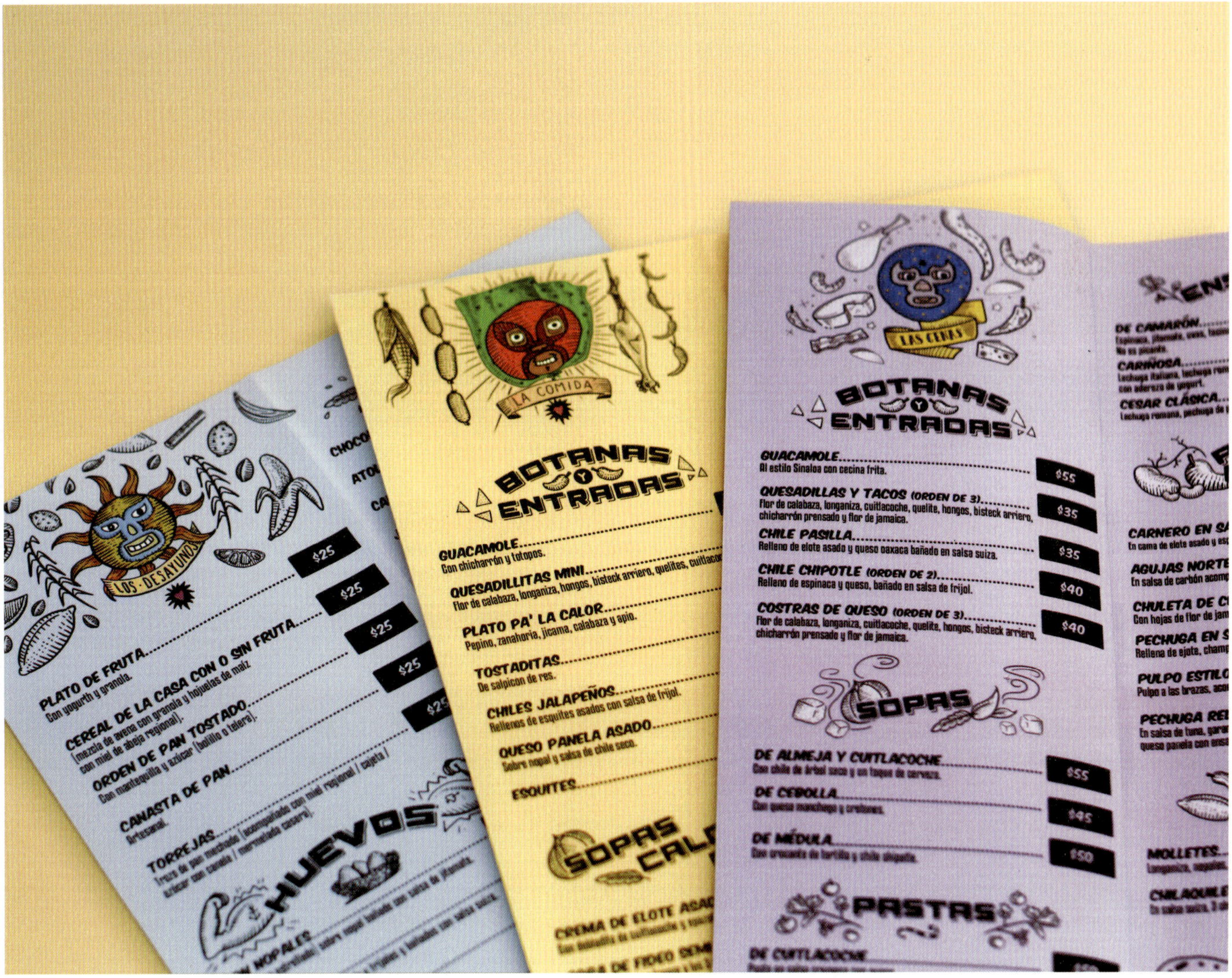

5 de mayo #165, Barrio de la Cruz, Centro Histórico, Querétaro, México

Studio: B3 Designers

Gymkhana

Gymkhana is an Indian restaurant and bar inspired by the colonial Indian clubs in the age of the British Raj. The visual image of the restaurant is a mix of Indian and British cultural and design references, conveying an exclusive upper class ambience of that particular period.

REGIONAL CUISINE

42 Albemarle Street, London, UK

Kricket

Kricket is a British Indian pop-up restaurant located in an old shipping container. The name is based on the sport (but written with a K) which is equally popular in both countries. The logo was inspired by Victorian lettering during the time of the Raj. The letter K also became a decorative element used for various wall-mounted screens which can be found in Indian architecture.

Studio: Mind Design
Illustrator: Lenia Hauser

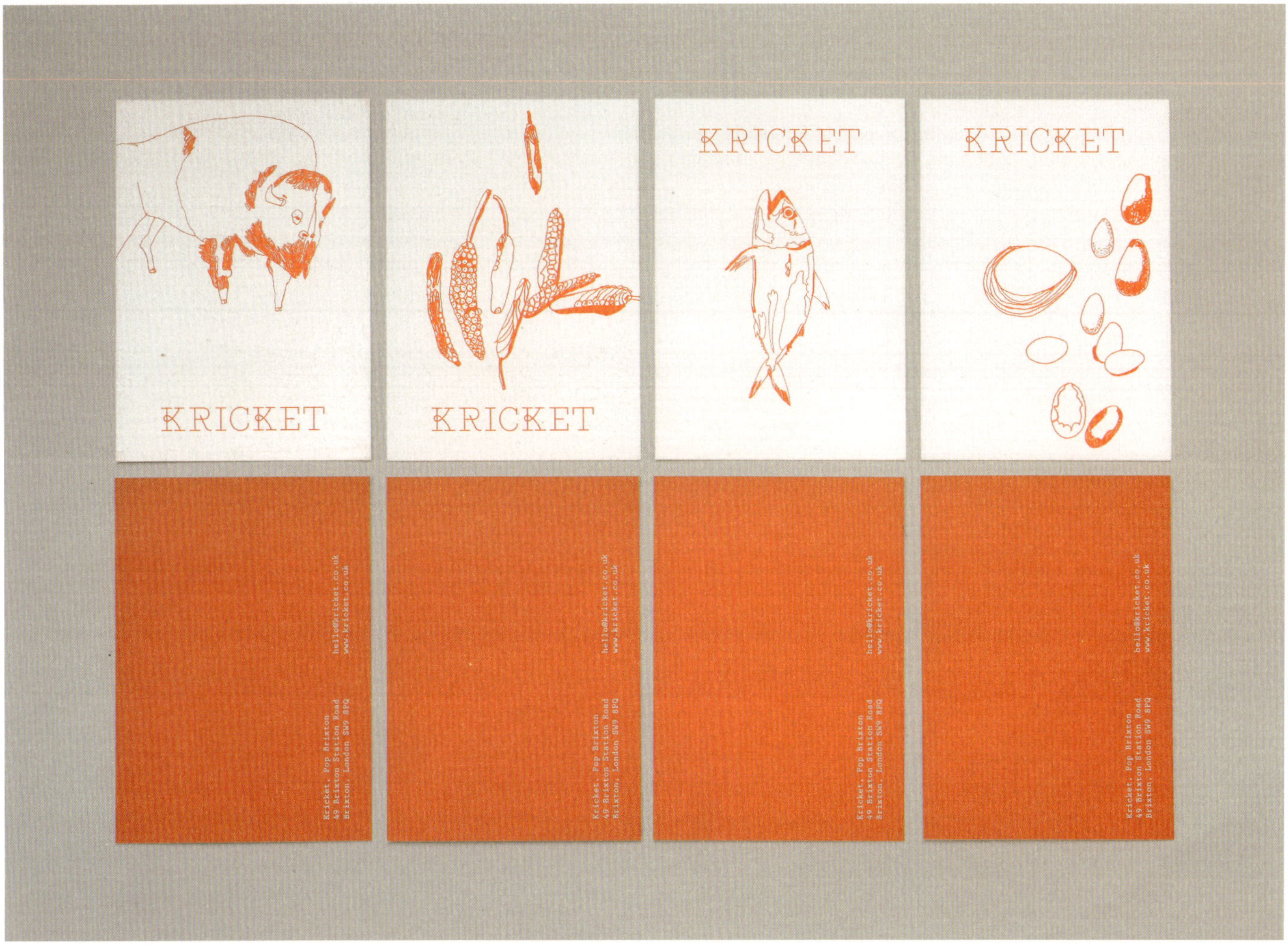

REGIONAL CUISINE

♦ Pop Brixton, 49 Brixton Station Road, London SW9 8PQ, UK

067

KHA

Kha is a relaxing bistro serving authentic Thai food including home-cooked selections from the chef's family recipes and a collection of innovated modern interpretation of Thai cuisine. The branding looks to the era of King Rama IV and King Rama V, both of whom had propelled the society of Siam forward through modernization. Researching on the archival articles of the Rattanakosin Kingdom during this period was an important step in creating this branding. The restaurant is positioned to be atypical from the usual Thai eateries: classy and elegant without the superfluous stereotypical Thai ornamental elements.

Studio: Foreign Policy
Creative Director: Yah-Leng Yu
Art Director: Yah-Leng Yu
Designer: Yah-Leng Yu
Logo Designer: Ammanda Choo

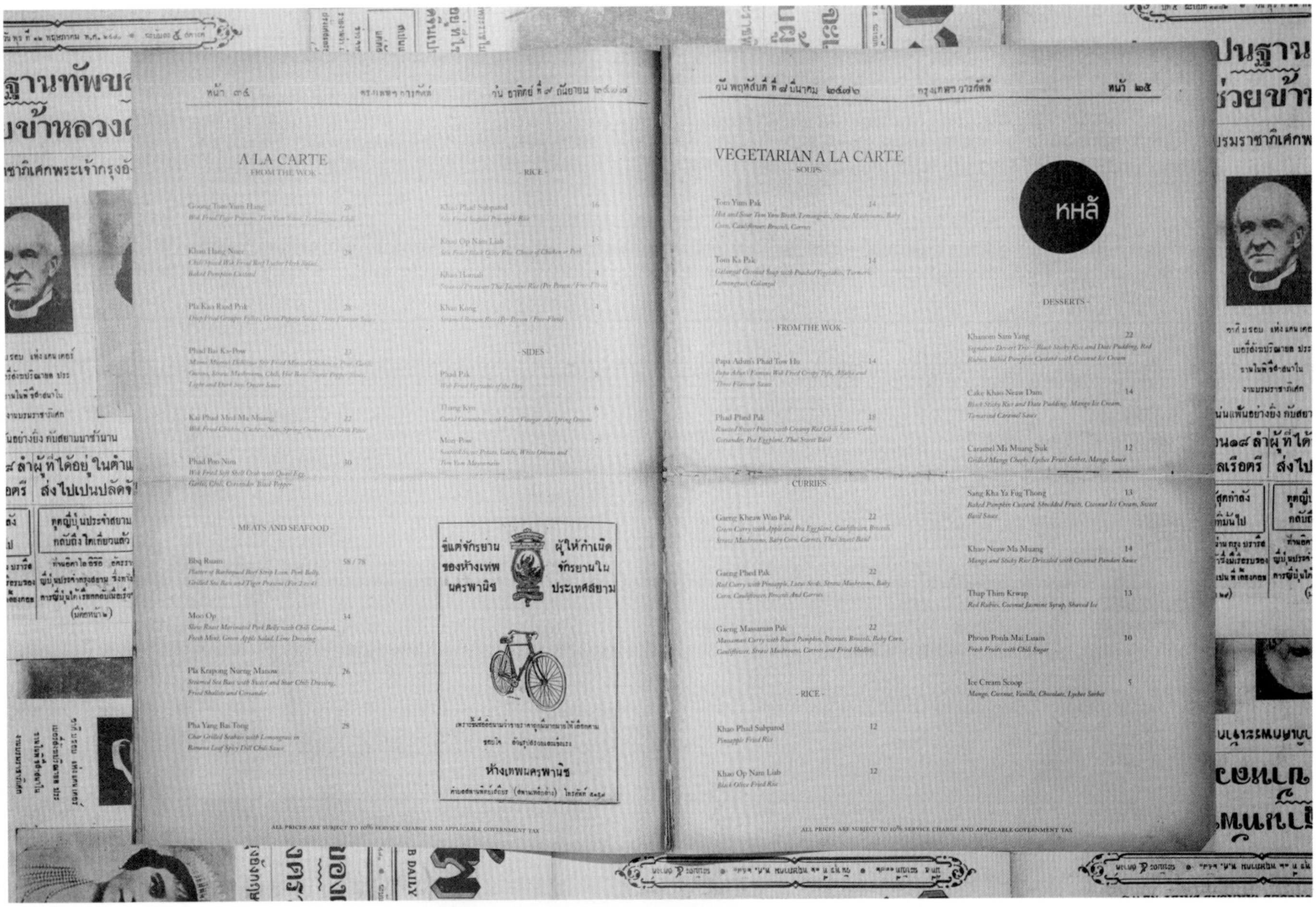

No.38 Martin Road, Singapore

Le Garçon Saigon

Le Garçon Saigon is a Vietnamese restaurant located in the quiet and upscale Star Street neighborhood. It celebrates the young, the quirky and the romantic in everything from its design to the menu itself. Brought to life through a palette of pastel roses and bold greens, the restaurant adopts the allure of a distinctly Parisian dining experience from the 1950s: open views, fine wine, strong coffee and dreamy conversations.

Studio: Substance

G/F, 12-18, Wing Fung St., Wan Chai, Hong Kong

Sassy's Red

The type, as the major element in the identity, pays homage to Jazz posters and reflects the collection of different dishes offered. Images of ladies from old postcards are also reflective of the Jazz era but highlight the Sassy concept. The business cards design took reference from old concert tickets printed on uncoated heavyweight stock, presented in strips and have perforated edges. The menu reflects the eclectic nature with every element being referenced from a different place.

Studio: The Creative Method
Creative Director: Tony Ibbotson
Designer: Andri Mondong

Level 5, shop 5002, Westfield Sydney, 188 Pitt st, Australia

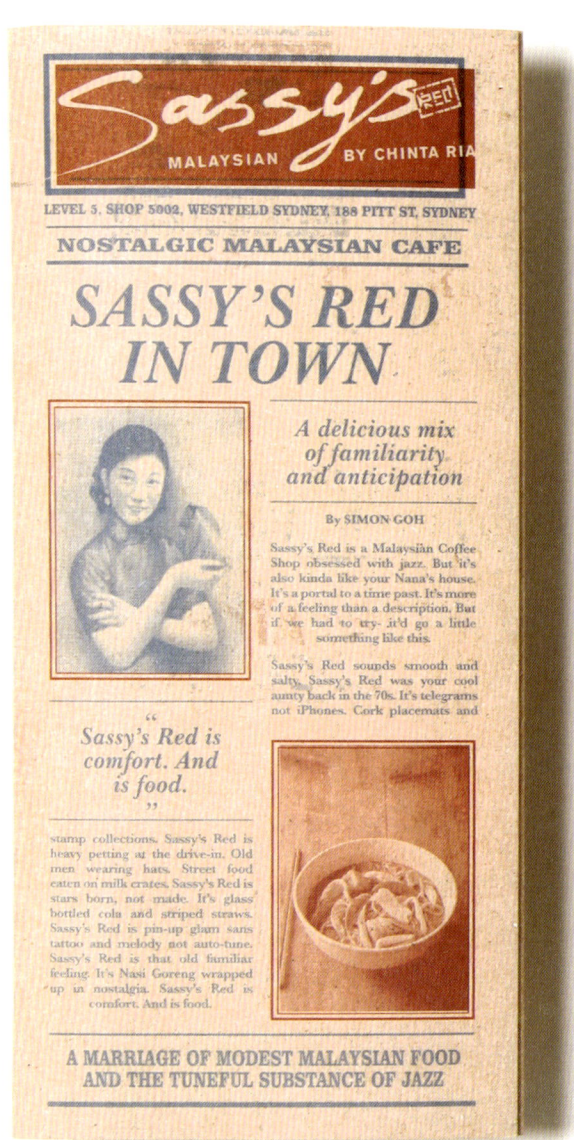

REGIONAL CUISINE

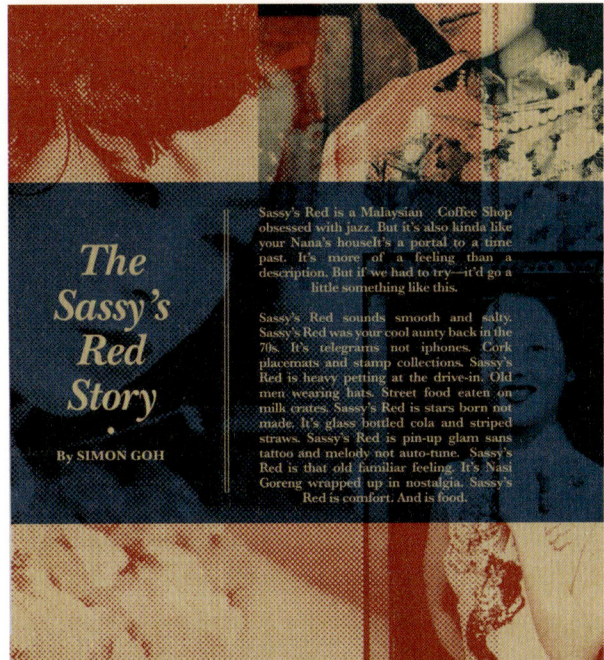

The Sassy's Red Story

By SIMON GOH

Sassy's Red is a Malaysian Coffee Shop obsessed with jazz. But it's also kinda like your Nana's house. It's a portal to a time past. It's more of a feeling than a description. But if we had to try—it'd go a little something like this.

Sassy's Red sounds smooth and salty. Sassy's Red was your cool aunty back in the 70s. It's telegrams not iphones. Cork placemats and stamp collections. Sassy's Red is heavy petting at the drive-in. Old men wearing hats. Street food eaten on milk crates. Sassy's Red is stars born not made. It's glass bottled cola and striped straws. Sassy's Red is pin-up glam sans tattoo and melody not auto-tune. Sassy's Red is that old familiar feeling. It's Nasi Goreng wrapped up in nostalgia. Sassy's Red is comfort. And is food.

Idol Restaurant

Guiyang is a sleepless city with bars, cafés and nightclubs everywhere. Late-night snacks or meals are therefore much in demand. While street food is believed to be unwholesome despite its low price, Idol restaurant runs a long hour opening and boasts its signature dish Spicy Crab which has attracted a great many late-night food hunters. Incorporating the night street food culture and the finger-guessing game, the designer based the branding on symbolic neon signs that could be further developed for other occasions.

Designer: Hongchang Shi, Biao Xiong

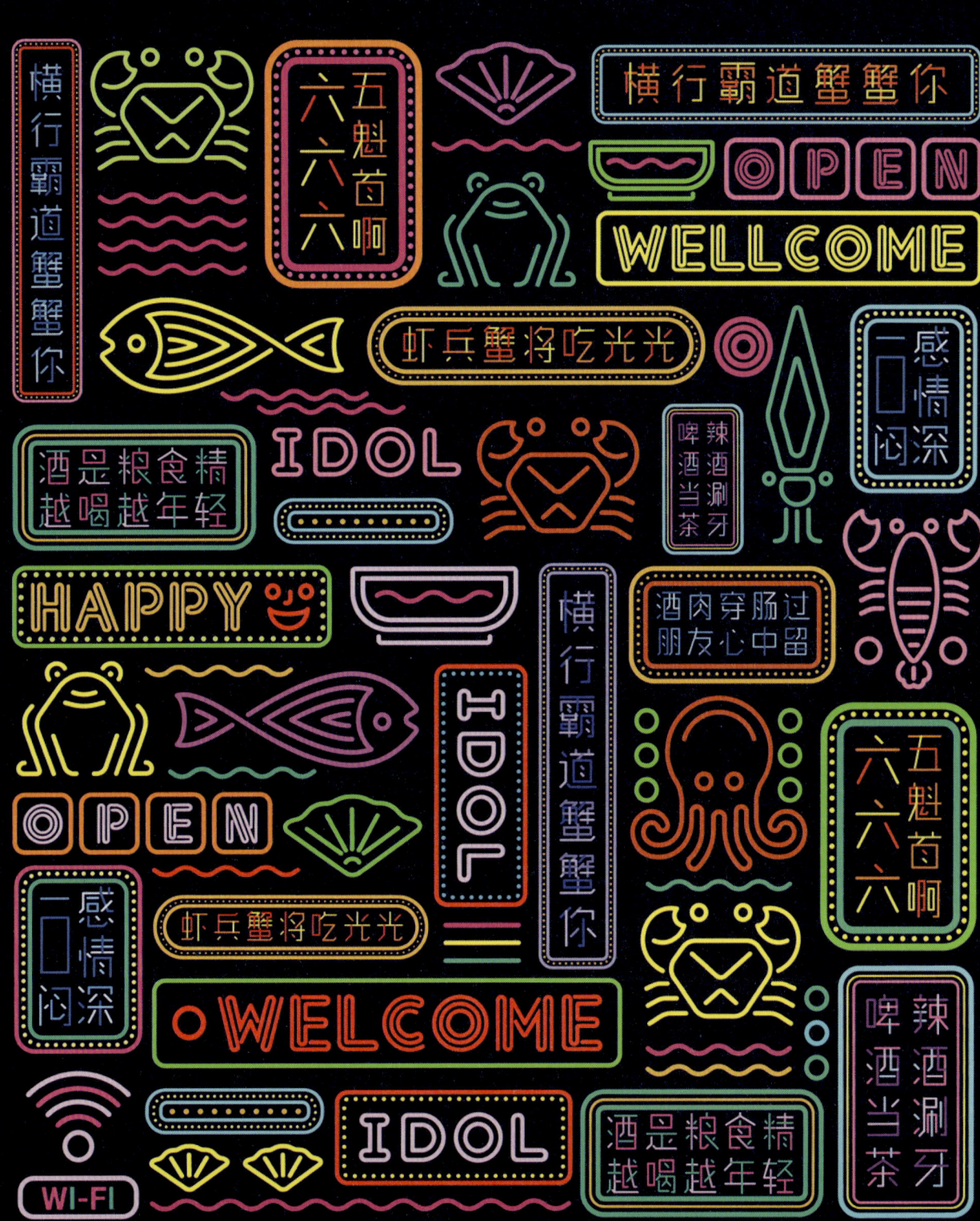

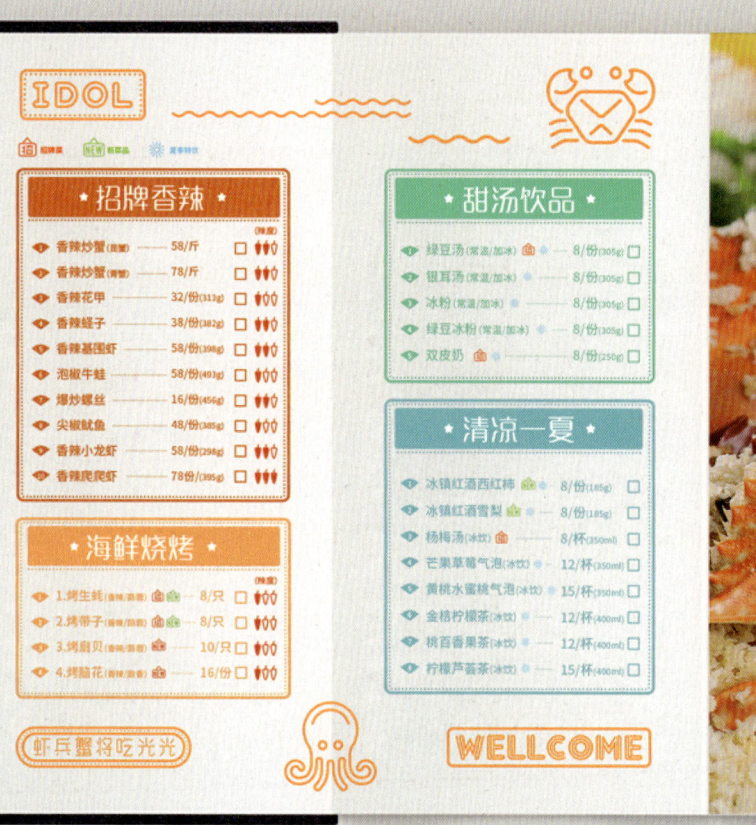

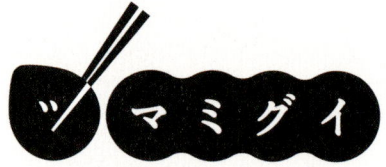

Tumamigui

The restaurant name "tumamigui" refers to an unrestricted pick-and-eat style of dining. Tablet device has been introduced to allow orders to be customized. There is a wide range of options including the amount of rice and wasabi, the size of seafood pieces, and other toppings and sauces. Raindrop shape is the basic element in the design system, from logo and pattern to the shape of the table. Each table's color combination and furniture is different in order to offer each customer a unique dining experience.

Studio: nendo

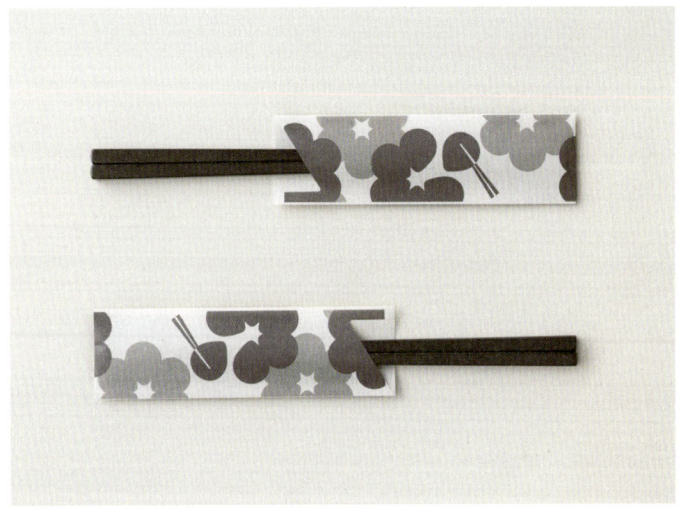

1-30-10 Aobadai, Meguro-ku, Tokyo-to 153-0042, Japan

Studio: FUTURA

RAW

Raw is a sushi bar that follows traditional Japanese cuisine art and its high quality standards. The branding preserves some classic elements such as the vintage imagery. The monochromatic color scheme, the Arabic and Japanese typography, and the brushstrokes that form the name "RAW" share a masculine personality countered by the delicacy of the dishes they offer. The tableware design features the use of Kintsugi, a Japanese way of repairing broken pottery with powdered gold, silver or platinum.

RAW SUSHI BAR

Mikôto

Mikôto is a new restaurant in the heart of Stuttgart. The design system has incorporated the art of Japanese calligraphy—Shodo, the highlighted gold lettering and the fish scales pattern that emphasizes the wide variety of fish offered in the restaurant. A cubic grid winds its way through the entire concept, from prints to interior design. Apart from this, the use of fish scales and the color gold and lilac also supports the consistency of the brand image.

Studio: ADDA STUDIO
Creative Director: Christian Vögtlin
Designer: Christian Vögtlin, Nadine März
Photographer: Melanie März

Tübinger Str. 41–43, 70178 Stuttgart, Germany

Thanks on the Table

Thanks on the Table is a new family run restaurant that serves seasonal and local foods. Developed on the concept of a family or friends sharing food and thoughts on one table, canaria created a cozy and festive image characterized by a minimal table icon. The logo has been used to form a particular pattern for the restaurant's floor.

Studio: canaria inc.
Designer: Yuji Tokuda, Toshikazu Minatomura, Mariko Yamasaki

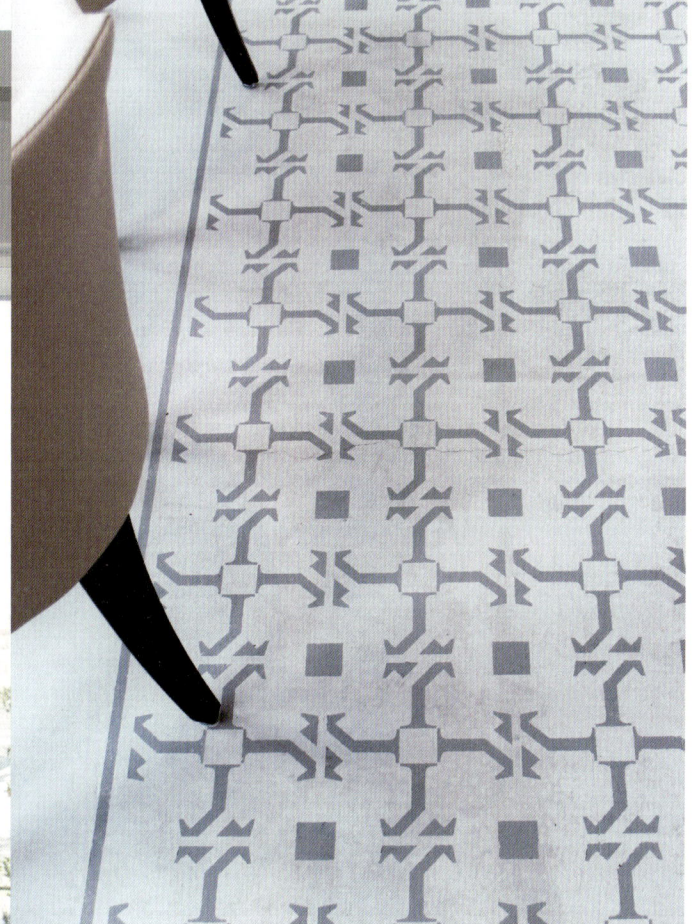

6-20-1,Tsujido-motomachi, Fujisawashi, Kanagawaken, Japan (inside Shonan T-SITE)

4ECK

The name 4eck refers to the "four corners" the restaurant physically resides, and also the "four corners" of the world. The new direction for their kitchen is based on the embrace of diverse cultures. Every meal on the menu was inspired by one city. Customers can go on a culinary journey around the globe. Based on this concept, the interior features miniature taxis from different cities, and cans carrying the names of cities.

Studio: kissmiklos
Exterior designer: Viktor Csap, kissmiklos
Photographer: Bálint Jaksa
Web Programmer: Atom&Partners

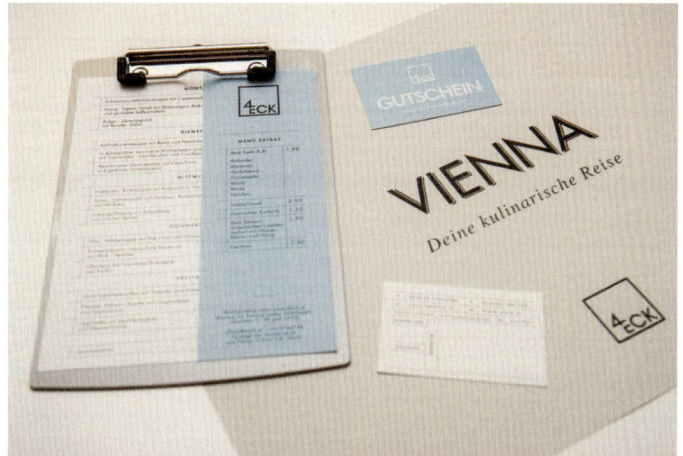

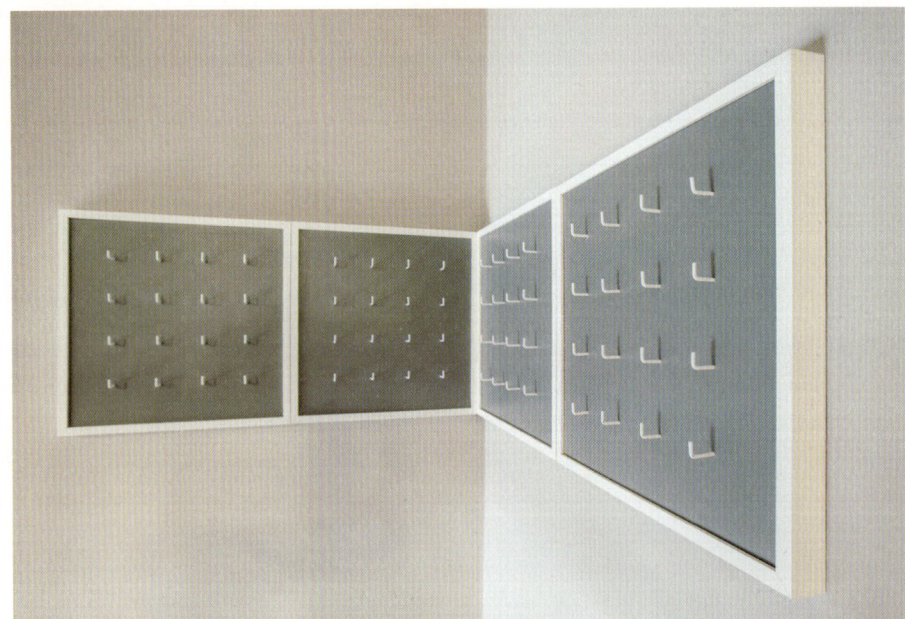

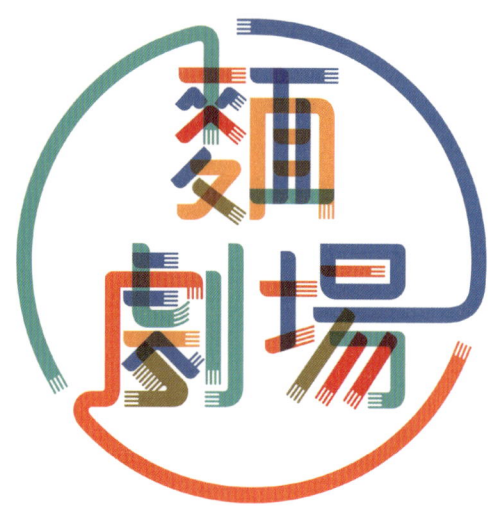    

Studio: Pentagram

Noodle Theater

Noodle Theater is a new restaurant chain in Taiwan serving regional noodle dishes from around the globe. The identity features a bold color palette that alludes to the restaurant's multicultural offerings and diversity of ingredients. The typographic logo comprises layered noodle-like strands that spell out Noodle Theater's name in Chinese characters. The colorful identity extends to a series of international masks, each representing a unique culture. The masks—including a Mexican luchador mask, a Japanese noh mask, and a British Guy Fawkes mask—are arranged as a striking graphic pattern and applied to the shop packaging, tableware, print materials, and environmental graphics.

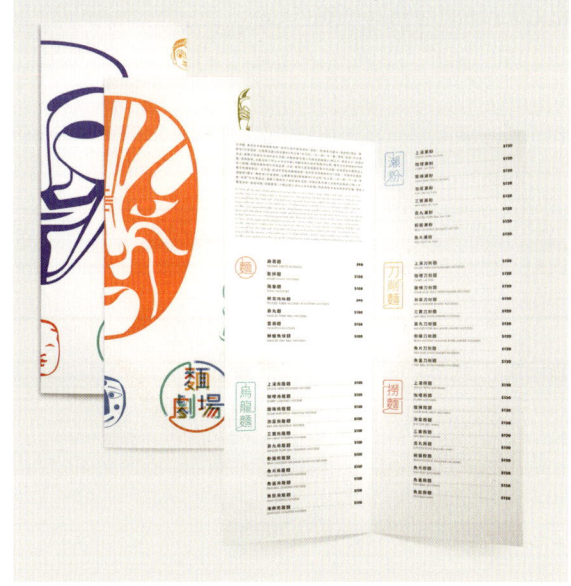

No.15, Aly.27, Ln.216, Sec.4, Zhong Xiao East Road, Da'an District, Taipei, Taiwan

099

Corner House

Corner House is a two-story black and white bungalow located in the Singapore Botanic Gardens. The restaurant serves contemporary cuisine "Gastro-Botanica" created by Chef Jason Tan. The branding was based on different inspirations—E.J.H. Corner, a botanist who used to live there, the charming house, the gardens and the botany. The story of the restaurant was incorporated to develop a refined and visually rich brand that covers a full range of design applications.

Studio: ONO CREATES
Creative Directors: Med & Jing
Photographer: John Heng
Communications Agency: Gastro-Sense

MIU Creative Cuisine

MIU is a vibrant and creative urban food and beverage brand specialized in creative rice dishes. It boasts a fusion of Eastern and Western rice ball recipes and natural ingredients. The design team based the identity on one key element—the Chinese character of rice, which is so flexible and versatile that different patterns have been developed to enrich the visuals.

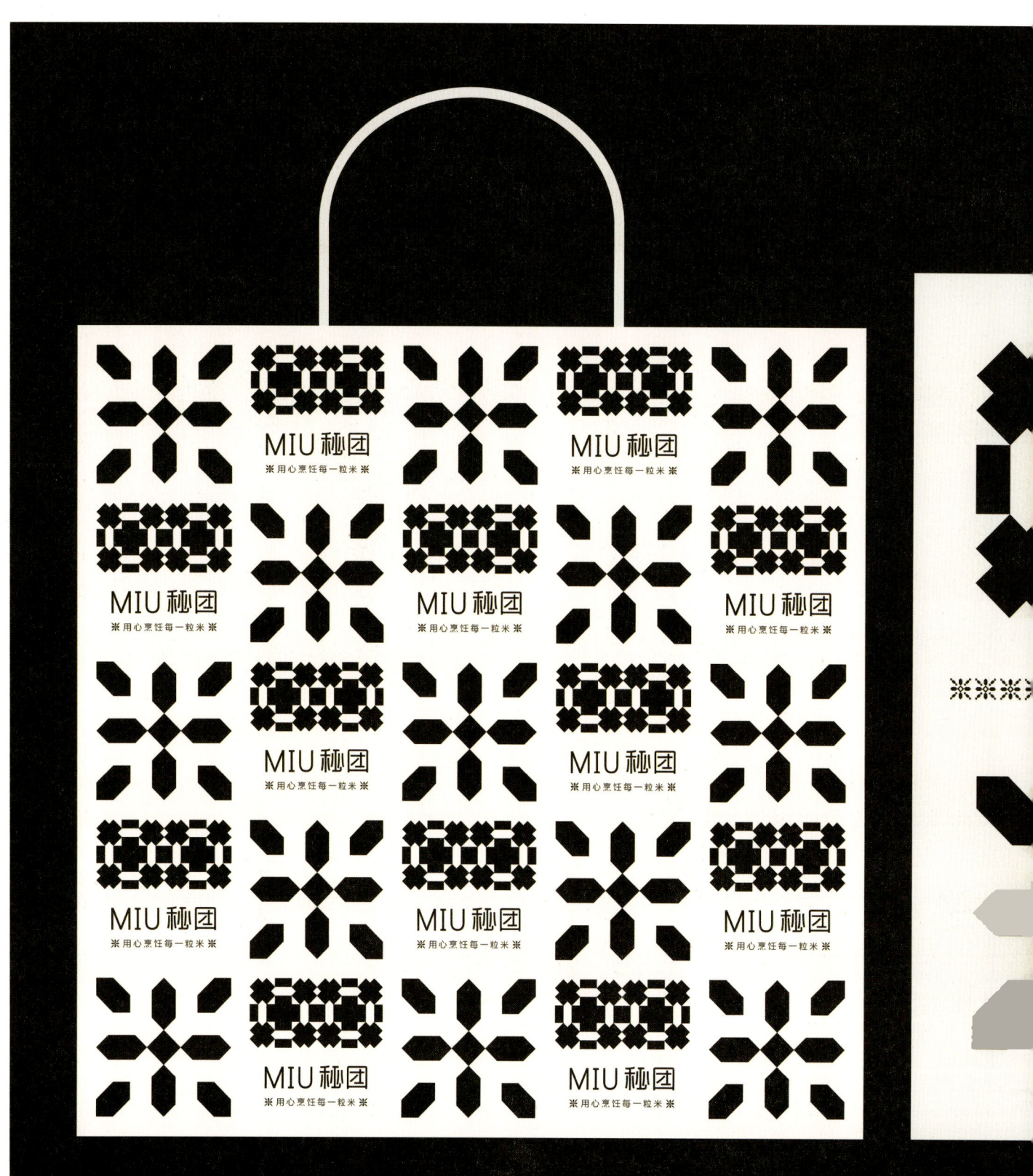

Studio: ONE & ONE DESIGN
Designer: Li Wen

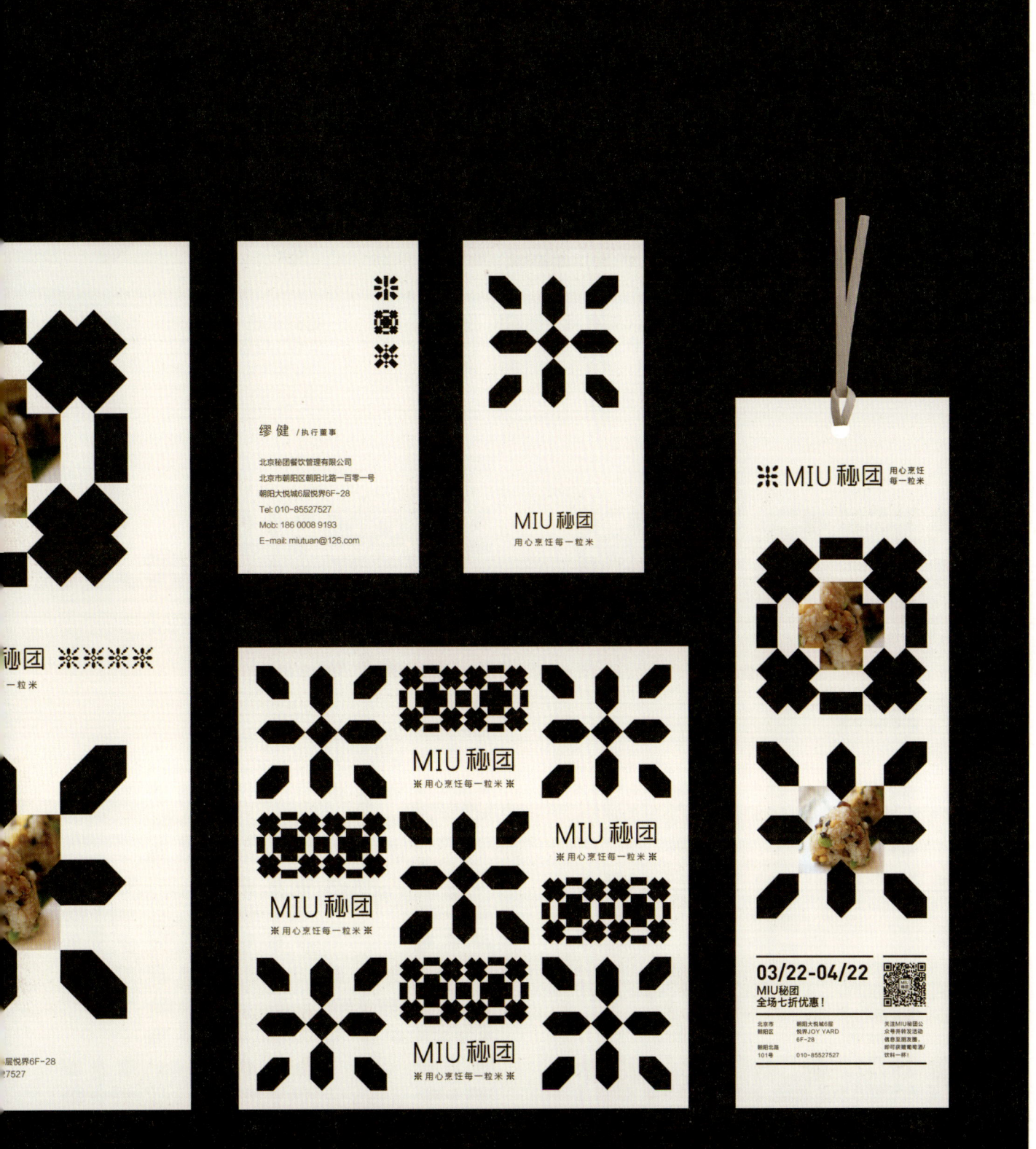

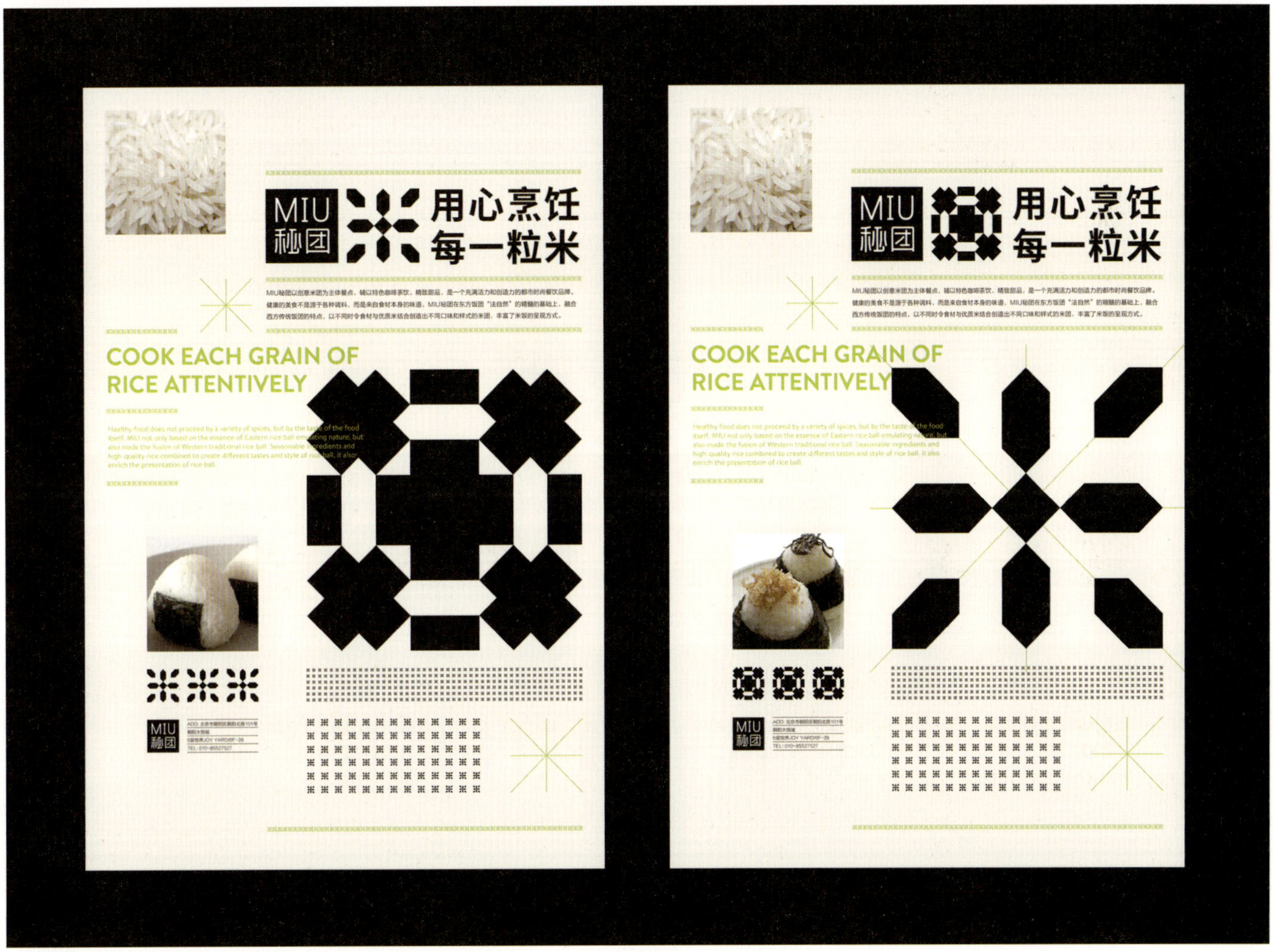

Catch and Release

Inspired by Chef Jason Neroni's youth spent on the East Coast, this seafood restaurant is a modern take on traditional New England style food. Catch and Release uses the only freshest catch sourced from the coast. A unique fish index flap sets its menu apart from the rest. The brand pairs colorful sea animal illustrations and lined-notepad-style menus to create an eye-catching system for the tasty cuisine.

Studio: Farm Design
Designer: Aaron Atchison, Braden Wise, Christine Gonda

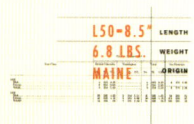

DEDICATED TO THE PROTECTION AND PURITY OF OCEAN TO TABLE SELECTION.

SHUCK YEAH.

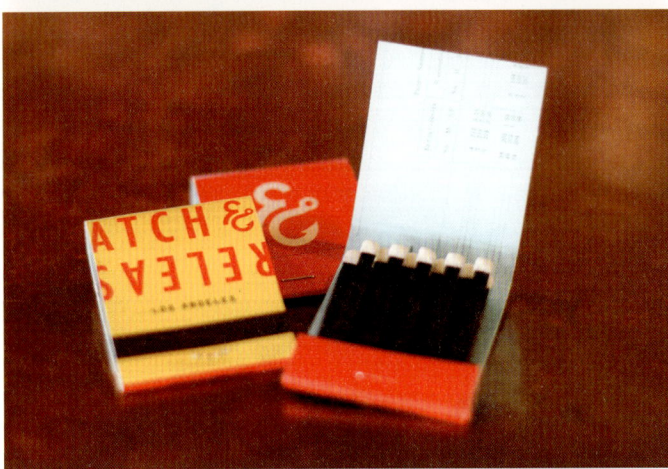

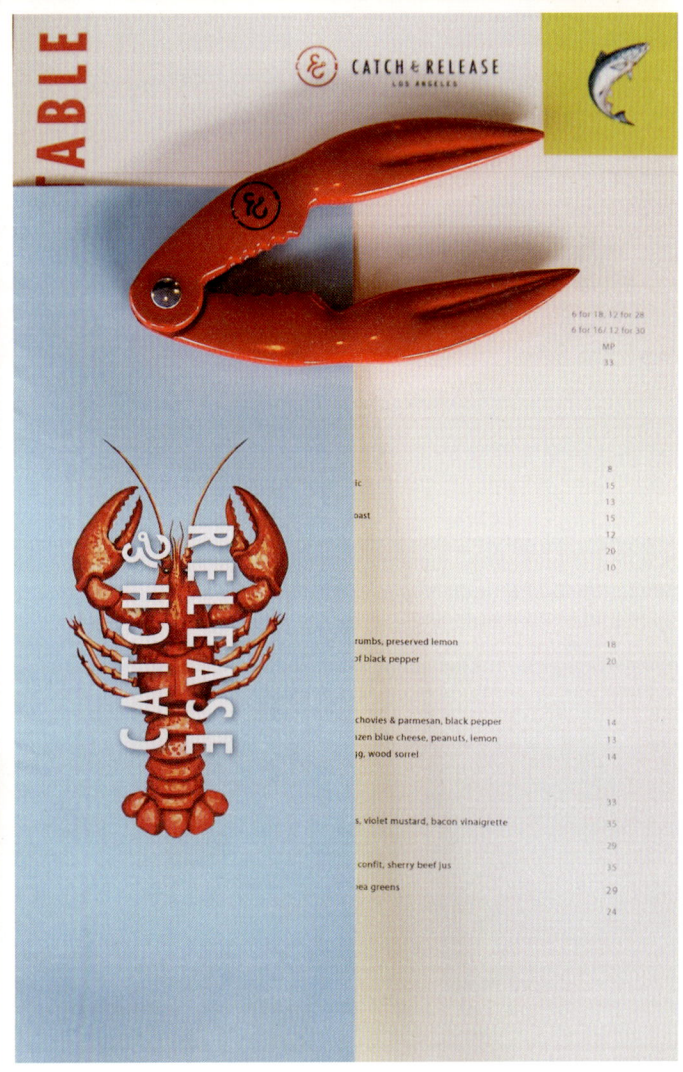

CATCH & RELEASE

DATE: JULY 15
LOCATION: MARINA DEL REY
WATER TEMP: 69°F
MIGRATION:
PRECIPITATION: 0%
WAVE COND: 2.6 FT / 13 SEC
WIND SPEED: 1-10 MPH

✳ DINE LA ✳

OYSTERS:
— BLUE POINT (CT)
— SALUTATION COVE (PEI)

SEAFOOD

Studio: Foreign Policy
Creative Director: Yah-Leng Yu
Art Director: Yah-Leng Yu
Designer: May Lim

The Pelican

The Pelican is a seafood dining space inspired by the comfort and celebratory spirit of sailors returning to land after a long voyage. The graphic of mixing human characters with sea animals was inspired by the dual functions of the restaurant. In the evening The Pelican transforms from a dining space to a bar. This blurring boundary between a restaurant and a bar led to the graphical interpretation of blurring the boundary between what is real and what is imaginary.

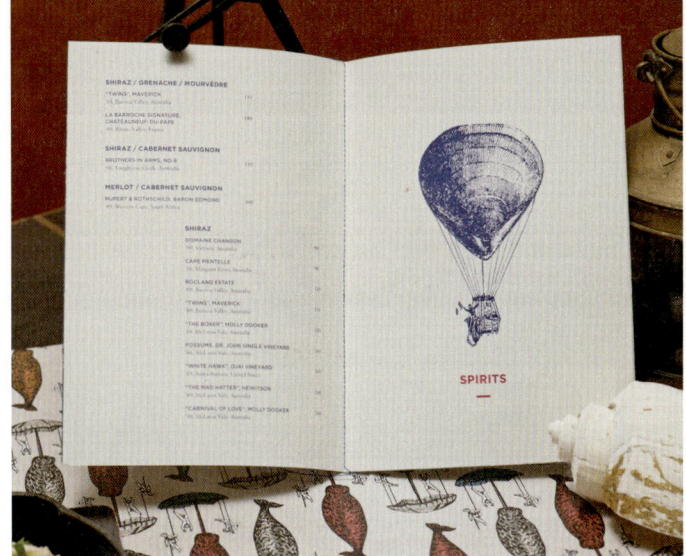

J1 Fullerton Road, #01-01, One Fullerton, Singapore

The Ocean

The initials of Ocean Club have constituted the restaurant's dynamic logo, with its geometrical purity strictly preserved. The interior invites customers through a pool of dark blues and cyan, balanced with sandy brown finishes throughout. Ceiling-to-floor windows offer a clear panoramic view of the seaside on the horizon, diving into the deep through the portal frames flourished with silver leaves. The tableware and furnishings took design cues from coral reefs, anemone spirals and Fibonacci sequence in shells—each designed to reflect the undersea organic geometry.

Studio: Substance
Photographer: Dennis Lo, Substance

SEAFOOD

303-304, 3/F, 28, The Pulse, Beach Rd, Repulse Bay, Hong Kong

115

Oyster´s & Co

The corporate identity project for the oyster bar covers art direction, brand design, packaging, photography and web design. Inspired by classic Mediterranean aesthetics, the graphic design is based on still life pencil sketches. creating an innovative and fresh image touched with a classic tenderness.

Studio: MONOTYPO Studio
Designer: Daniel Barba López
Photographer: Diana Cristina Espinoza
Web Programmer: Carlos Pesina

SEAFOOD

Tepeyac 1042 colonia chapalita, zapopan jalisco, Mexico

119

Simple.

Simple. is a new generation fast-food restaurant. The idea of the restaurant is "be simple, eat simple" implying cooking with local, fresh, non-preserved products in unusual combinations. Based on this concept, the design team adopted natural colors and simple materials like wood, plywood, craft paper, etc. without complicated refinement. A shovel was used as a door-handle, rakes as coat hooks, rolling pins as a menu for drinks, recycled bottles as lamps and so on.

Studio: Brandon
Creative Director: Boris Alexandrov
Designer: Elena Parhisenko, Olga Novikova, Anton Storozhev
Interior Designer: Anna Domovesova
Copywriter: Dmitriy Panasiuk

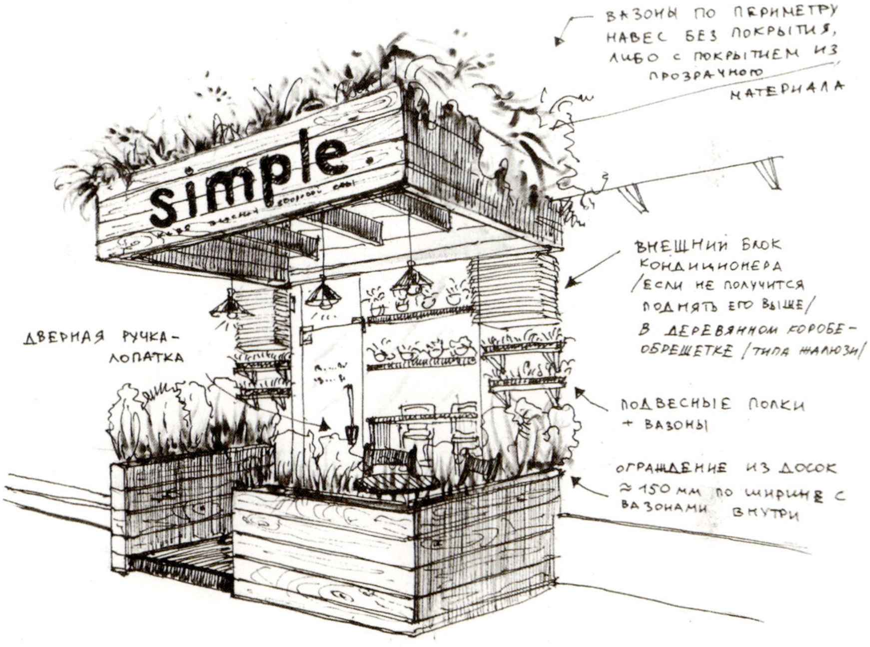

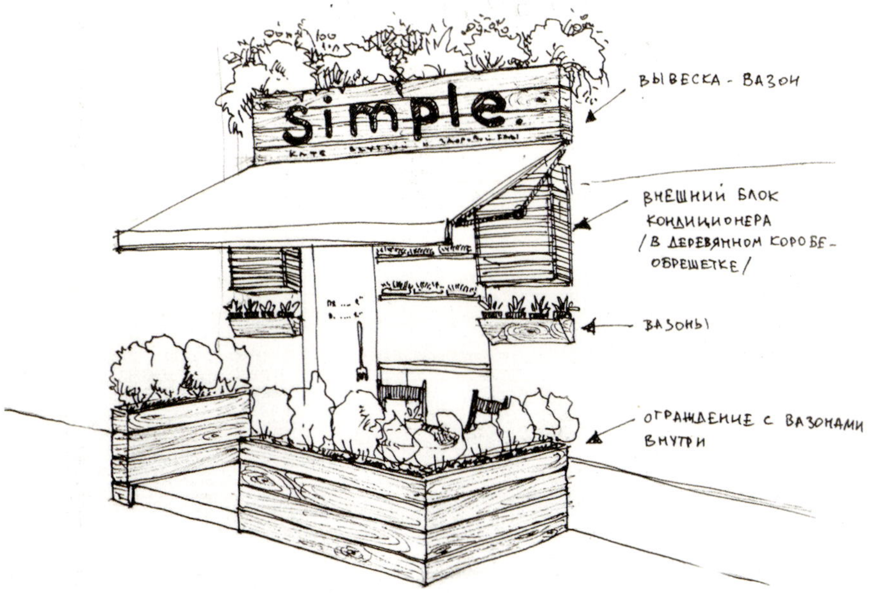

Botánica

Botánica is a food delivery and takeout store, selling home-made style sandwiches and salads among other things. The studio tried to present this concept with the use of mild and draft fonts, photo shooting of production in natural light and vintage illustrations. A very interesting texture that reminds people of natural elements such as wood or earth helped create an abstract form for the identity. This texture is a very important element in the whole system becasuse of its strong character.

Studio: Bunker3022
Art Director: Vanya Silva
Designer: Vanya Silva, Carolina Sosa
Photographer: Mercedes Monti

Iberá 1643, Nuñez, Buenos Aires, Argentina

Mary Wong

Mary Wong is a chain of noodle bars, where noodle is made with Asian accuracy and American spirit. The branding was oriented towards a modern and minimalistic style. Different from the conventional Asian themes in design, concrete walls, metal furniture and neon lights are combined to generate a metropolis night atmosphere. The vivid colored stickers serve both as part of the identity and markers of the main ingredients.

Studio: Fork
Designer: Kirill Ermoshin, Ivan Maximov, Pavel Platonov

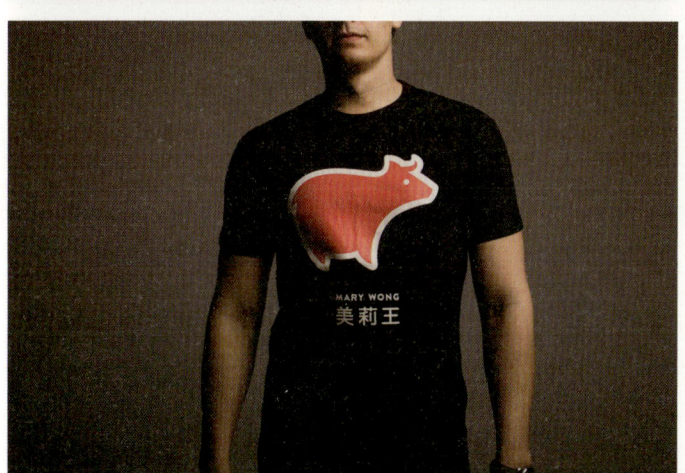

Pig's Pearls

This identity project for the gourmet burger restaurant borrowed the graphic style from the Victorian age and the English engraving from the late nineteenth century. A pig wearing a crown in the logo is a humorous touch to the vintage style. The opaque black product containers have greatly elevated the brand image with distinct characteristics. The label design was inspired by a golden age of graphic arts when the American Sanborn Maps, wood typefaces and Spaghetti Western movies flourished.

Studio: MONOTYPO Studio
Designer: Daniel Barba López
Photographer: Diana Cristina Espinoza
Web Programmer: Carlos Pesina

· MEMORIA DE AYER ·

SABORES DE HOY

THE ONLY ONE **001** THE ONLY ONE

Studio: Mast
Designer: Manuel Astorga, Rodrigo Aguadé

Holly Burger

The restaurant is named after Holly who was the aunt of the restaurant owner and the creator of the many secret burger recipes. The task was to create a real American-style brand with a fresh mix of style references. The inspiration came from various vintage, hand-drawn American typographies on the old shop windows and banana leaf wallpaper that had been originally designed in 1942 by decorator Don Loper for the Beverly Hills hotel in Los Angeles, California.

Studio: Substance
Photographer: Dennis Lo

Burger Circus

Burger Circus is a whimsical take on the classic late 19th century Americana diner. The space, inspired by Edward Hopper's painting "Compartment C, Car 293", encompasses train carriage accents like the curved stainless steel wall panels and warm tones casted by vintage lamps. The circus narrative in the branding content was derived from the movie *Water for Elephants* and practiced throughout the menus and posters which vividly display the different characters' quirks and talents.

Burger & Love

The main design concept comes from the fact that burger was born from the street of America, and became one of the favorite symbols of pop art. Motivated by a pop art exhibition, the designer launched a "Pop" restaurant branding in a modern context, with the interior in the iconic style from 1950s and 1960s.

Studio: kissmiklos
Exterior designer: Viktor Csap, kissmiklos
Photographer: Bálint Jaksa

Burger House

Bond was tasked with the re-branding and interior design for a chain of burger restaurants in Abu Dhabi. Assembling a local team of designers and producers while working with interior designers from Bond Helsinki, the team freshened up the interior and developed a modern logo with vivid colors, which is a perfect match for Burger House's young and hip customers.

Studio: Bond

Al Muneera, Al Raha Beach, Opposite Etihad Complex, Al Raha, Abu Dhabi, UAE

Better Burger

This branding was based on Better Burger's candid manner and pursuit of original and impeccable dining experience. The hand drawn type and illustrations emphasize the source of the ingredients and reinforce the philosophy of making things better by hand. The result is an easily identifiable brand that promises and delivers a better burger.

Studio: 485 Design
Designer: James Showler

31 Galway Street, Auckland CBD, New Zealand / 19 Vulcan Lane, Auckland CBD, New Zealand

EL POLLERIO

El Pollerio

El Pollerio is new concept self-service chicken rotisserie that offers good quality food at an affordable price and a small number of items targeting at younger customers. The branding task included naming, graphic identity and interior design, under the four key words—fun, new, fresh, simple. The studio decided to create a pattern which works as the brand image and is recognizable even without the logo, and use white tiles for walls and silver ceiling that help to make the space appear larger and bright.

Studio: Is Creative Studio
Creative Director: Richars Meza

Avenida Antonio Sucre 1099, Lima 15084, Peru

Pelman Hand Made Café

The old school style and the mustache man character have been Pelman's distinguishing features. The interior is defined by wall decoration of oak, illustration, cutting boards and rolling pins, and a restored metal staircase with mosaic inscriptions.

Studio: G-sign
Photographer: Nikita Kryuchkov

FAST FOOD

Da Pizza Project

The most amazing thing about this cozy pizzeria is that customers can create their own pizzas. The first step is to choose a crust size and add cheese and tomato sauce, and then pick ingredients from classic pepperoni to things as exotic as pork chicharrones. Through the contrasting graphic elements—colors, 3D cheese lettering and the images of fresh ingredients—along with the slogan "Do It Yourself", the identity communicates the infinite options Da Pizza Project offers.

Studio: Jerome & Zimmerman
Designer: Ana Lorena Amaya, Luis De Hoyos, Antonio Rodriguez, Andrés Amaya Daniela Berumen
Architecture: Noborders Collective, Adrian Lucio, Jose Carlos Gonzalez

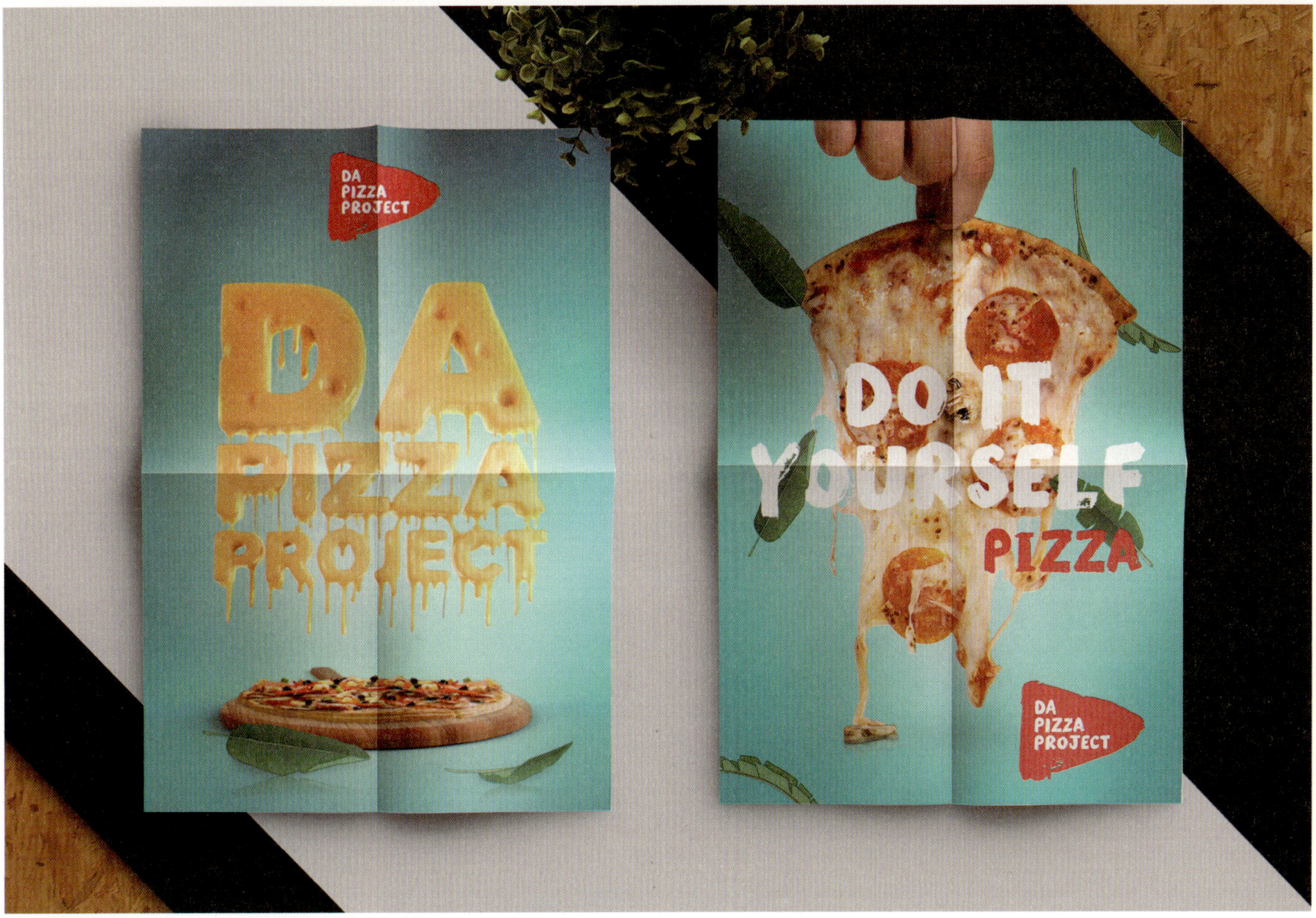

Río Mississipi #340, San Pedro Garza García, N.L. Mexico

Hotshot

The brand identity and interior design are direct reflections of fearless low-rider graffiti lifestyle of Hotshot. The restaurant's hangar interior is modeled around a lifeguard station, with iconic surfboards adorning the walls, vintage comics and classic beer crates. The materials used were chosen to reflect the easy-going aesthetic, incorporating sun-bleached wood, industrial corrugated steel surfaces, a bigass fan and bright neon signage. Every last detail, from the Airstream catering trailer to the comics on the menu, was custom-made and painstakingly crafted to transport customers back to a simpler, groovier time.

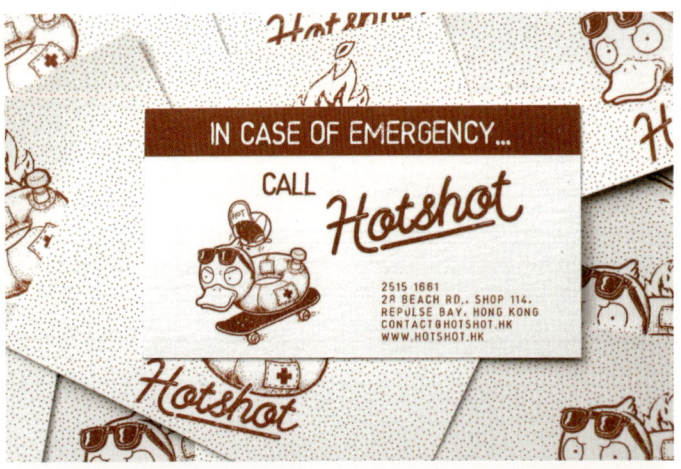

Studio: Substance

La Condesa

Breaking from traditional standards of delicatessens, La Condesa seeks to make visitors feel special. There are three areas that allow different sensations: the terrace is the place to spend a pleasant evening enjoying different dishes and drinks; the bar is the spot to meet people over cocktails or a selection of appetizers; the lounge with the sofas, mirrors on the ceiling and dim lighting create a magical and intimate atmosphere to spend the evening with good food.

Studio: PLASMA NODO
Photographer: Daniel Mejía

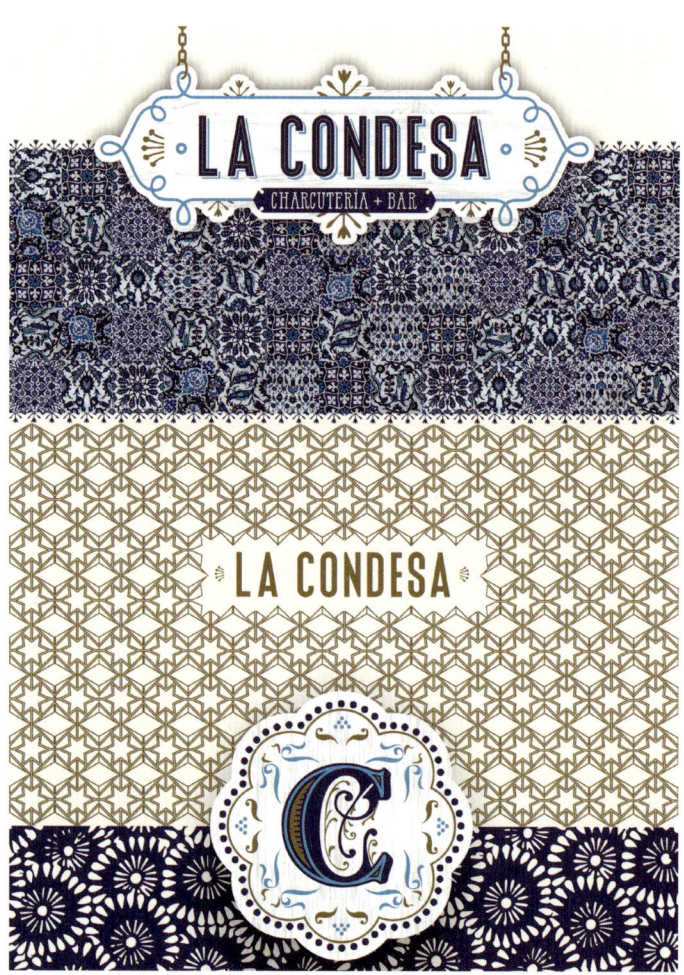

Carrera 36 # 10B - 78, Medellín, Colombia

Tamarindo

Tamarindo is a kitchen and bar with an international menu, created as a refreshing alternative for the locals. The identity's horizontal contrast of the colorless with three pastels and bright orange is neatly grounded on the restaurant's dual role as both a kitchen and a bar, bringing about a distinctive character as well as a strong consistency. The consistency is also reinforced with the material diversity, including the light wood for the menus, the linen of the tote bag and the glass of the jar.

Studio: La Tortillería
Designer: Rodrigo Véjar
Interior Design: Ruben Gil D., Gretta R. Valdés

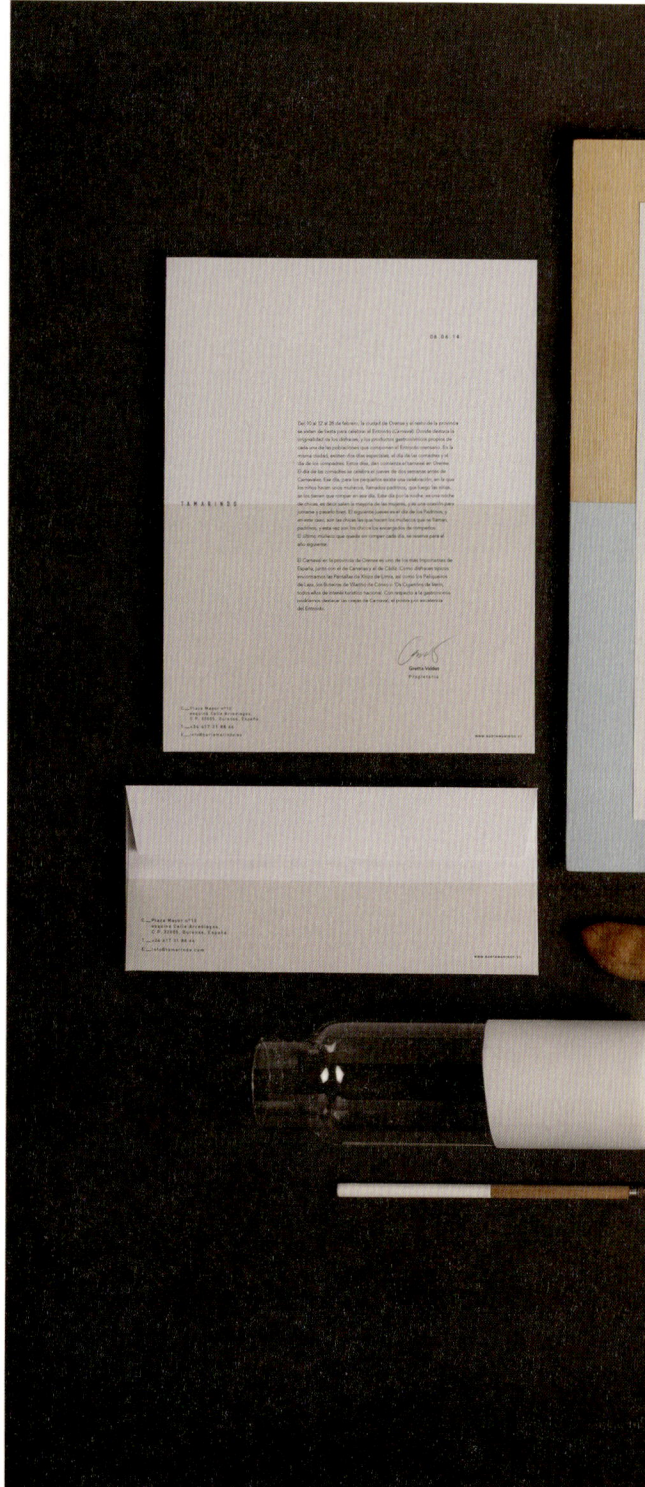

Kakhovka Bar

Most of the branding items such as business cards and tableware are hand-made for a better delivery of the nostalgic atmosphere of the first half of the 20th century. Tactile sensation plays an important role in the corporate style perception, and therefore wood, thick carton, thick felt and color loam are used.

Designer: Dmitry Neal
Illustrator: Evgeny Kalayanov
Photographer: Olga Queen

Turgeneva st.16, Orel, Russia

Sagrado

The identity illustrates the bar in two aspects: traditional way of eating and drinking; new way of sharing food and drink with whom we love. The logo is the key element to reflect these two aspects. The hand illustration inspired by painter Albrecht Dürer is followed by other graphic elements such as the serif font, the engravings and the sober color tones, corresponding to the bar interior. The other version of the logo made out of typography illustrates the innovative side of Sagrado, while the composition of the type maintains a classy vibe.

Designer: Gabriel Finotti, Solenn Robic
Photographer: Hick Duarte

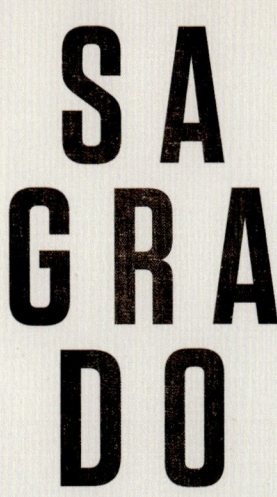

Una Kitchen & Microbrewery

The idea of brewing craft beer in small-scale production started in the USA more than ten years ago. Una is a brewery bar built on this trend: locally made beer and food in perfect harmony, with a focus on exceptional local ingredients. Una brings together craft beers from all over the world, as its name suggests "together" or "in one". The logo is designed as an ambigram, reflecting the essence of the corporate concept: togetherness.

Studio: KIND

KITCHEN AND BAR

Bryggen 7 NO-5003 Bergen, Norway

Santa Monica Yacht Club

Santa Monica Yacht Club is a bar focused seafood restaurant centered on handcrafted cocktails and small plates. Inspired by the symbolic nature of nautical flags, the brand speaks to one of the restaurant's favorite mantras—A rough day at sea is better than any day in the office. Award winning chef, Andrew Kirschner, updates the menu every evening as they only use the freshest and most local ingredients. Alongside the exquisite culinary experience, you will be pleased to discover the GPS coordinates on the menu are actually the current date.

Studio: Farm Design
Designer: Aaron Atchison, Braden Wise, Angela Kowalski

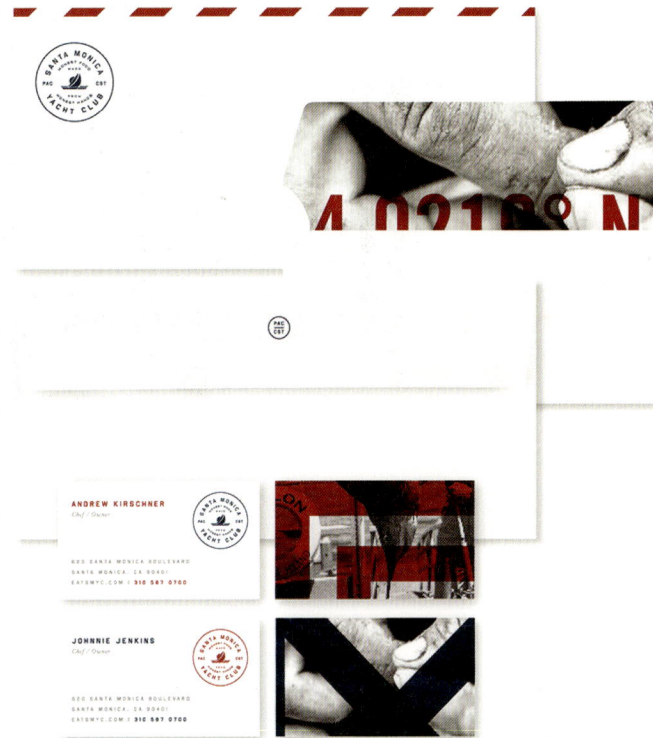

CUSTOM
COMMUNAL
TABLE

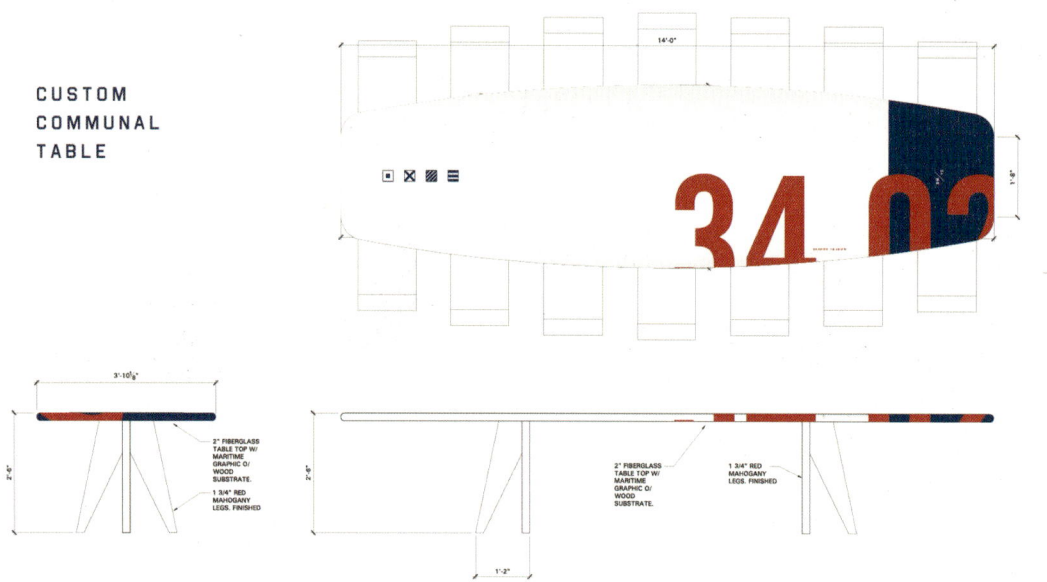

KITCHEN AND BAR

181

Puebla 109

This three-story 20th century townhouse is where art, design and gastronomy converge, in the forms of a restaurant, a bar and members club. The identity was developed around several symbols inspired by the classic age of Mexican philately to make up a rigid graphic system. The applications stand out with bold colors and classic typefaces that have a strong national character, along with other graphic elements that resemble those used by the postal system in the past.

Studio: Savvy
Interior: Marcela Lugo, Arturo Dib
Photographer: Coke Bartrina

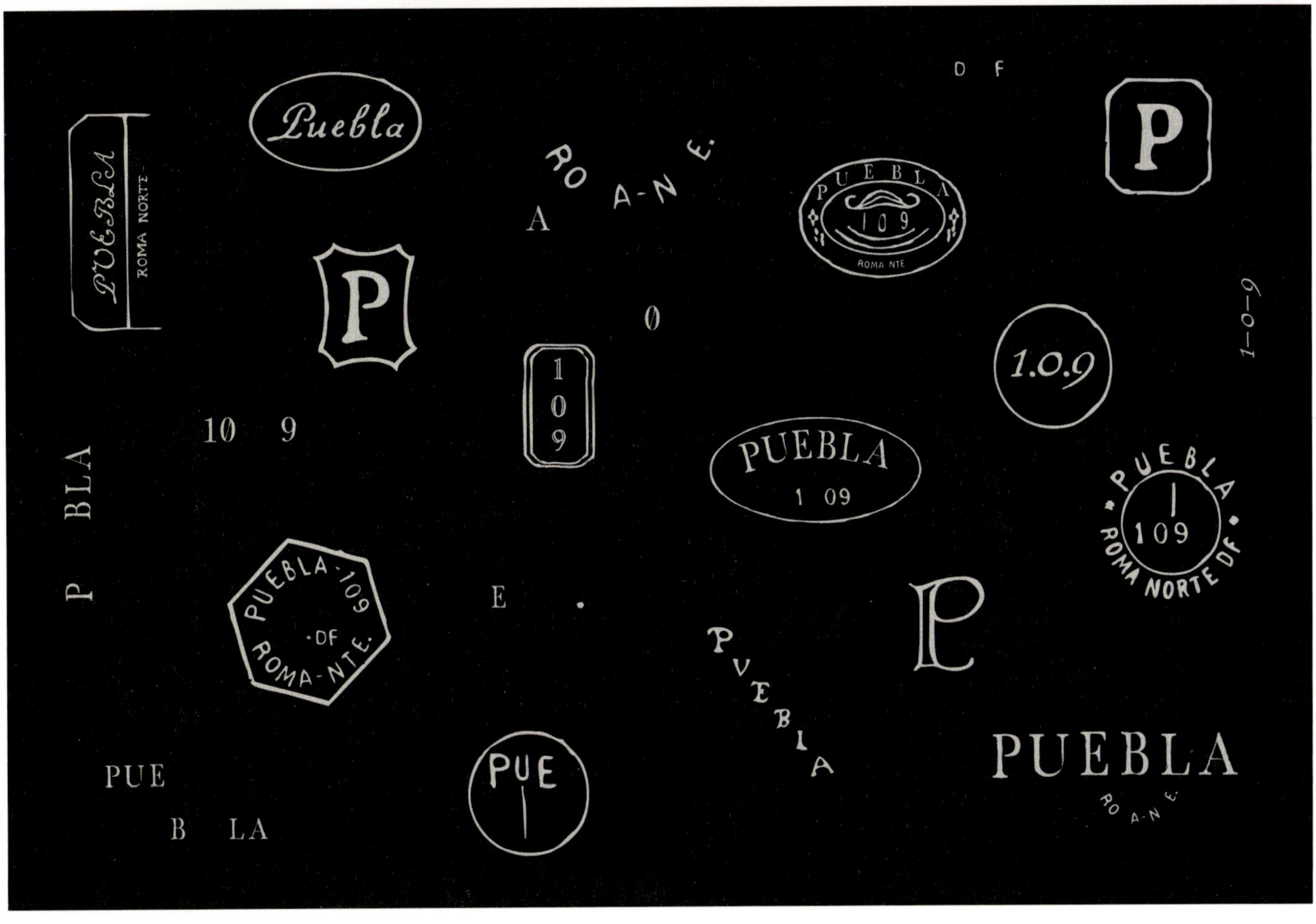

Puebla 109, col. roma norte, México, D.F. Mexico

Studio: United Design Practice
Photographer: Shawn Koh, Feng Studios

En Vain

This is the branding for a Chinese baijiu bar and restaurant aimed at the hip, the young and the fashionable. The Chinese alcoholic beverage baijiu is perceived to be for an older demographic and old fashioned. The design team has taken the opportunity to reinvent the category, in terms of how Chinese cultural elements can be interpreted in a fresh manner, yet respectful of its historical context. The name En Vain, French for "in vain", is a direct reference to this playful interpretation of the culture from food and drinks all the way through to design.

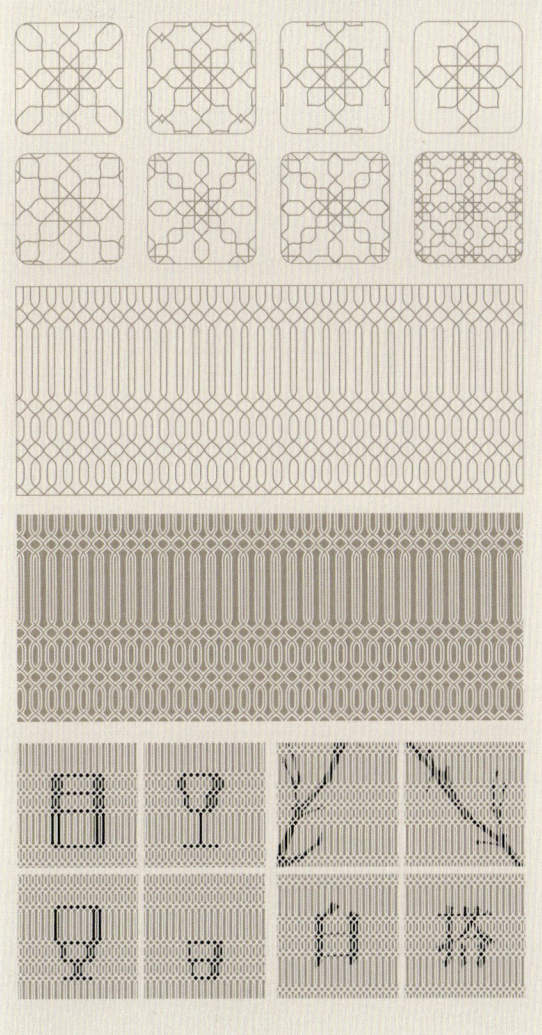

Mama Liu & Sons

Mama Liu & Sons is a family run restaurant and bar in Vienna, serving genuine Chinese dim sum and hot pot along with drinks. As the place has been passed down to the younger generation, the design team decided to deliver a modern image—clean layout and color combination throughout the prints and the interior. The traditional Chinese fresco in the interior is a hint of the authentic Chinese cuisine, with the embedded graffiti style corresponding to the design vibe.

Studio: Atelier Olschinsky

Banyan Bar & Refuge

Adam&Co. worked with The Gallows Group and developed the identity for their newest venture, Banyan Bar & Refuge. Banyan is a modern Asian gastro pub located in Boston's South End. The space features a large outdoor patio sheltered by the branches of nearby trees, which has inspired the branding concept. For the identity a rustic modern vibe was created to reflect Chef Phil Tang's approach to food.

Studio: Adam&Co.
Designer: Adam Larson

EAT

BANYAN

COLD AND RAW

Smoked scallop, asian pear, pickled celery	8
Fluke, toasted chili oil, orange, soy ginger, cashew	8
Spice cured salmon, pomegranate, coconut lime vinaigrette	12
Duxbury oysters, half dozen, black vinegar horseradish mignonette	8
Uni, brioche toast, pickled plums, lardo	8
Jonah crab claws, ginger scallion relish, burnt chili oil, lime	8
Seafood salad, mussel, shrimp, calamari, roasted green chili vinegar, cilantro	10
Beef tartare, kimchi, apple, fried capers, nori	11

RICE and NOODLES and BUNS

Cast iron duck fried rice, confit, cured breast, pickled shiitakes, gochujang ketchup, fried egg	14
Vegetable fried rice, asparagus, peas, morels, smoked tofu, fried egg, salsa verde	12
Warm lobster roll, steamed bread, honey miso butter, pickled celery	14
Fried oyster bun, garlic black bean aioli, arugula	14
Red braised pork bun, pickled mustard greens, fried shallots	14

VEGETABLES

Silken tofu, smoked shiitake mushrooms, toasted walnuts, crispy shallots	10
Lamb fat roasted potatoes, ground lamb, mint and cilantro, toasted rice powder	10
Pickled mushroom salad, king oyster, yellowfoot, poplar, daikon, asparagus	10
Carrot and kohlrabi salad, cured jalapenos, shiitake crumble	10
Stir fried market greens, housemade oyster sauce	10
Charred okra, mustard brown butter, chili threads, lemon	10

SNACKS

"Takoyaki", braised calamari, miso mayo, nori, bonito flake	8
Crispy pork wontons, fried chilies, smoked tahini	8
Kung pao sweetbreads, peanuts, sweet pepper jam, toasted chili oil	8
Smoked pork trotter croquette, hot mustard, apple frisee salad	8
Wild mushroom potsticker, parmesan frico, black vinegar reduction	8
Chicken liver mousse, pickled vegetables, mint, toasted baguette	8

FOR SHARING

ME mussel and pork belly crepe, pickled bean sprouts, mint and cilantro

Whole fried fish, spicy lime sauce, peppercorn salt, ginger scallion relish

Pork sausage platter, herb salad, nuoc cham, hot mustard, cabbage slaw, steamed bread

Marinated Strip Loin, kimchi butter, scallion pancakes, sauces and pickles

Spicy Fried Chicken, drums and thighs, charred lemon chimichurri, kewpie mayo

Potato salad

GRILLED

Japanese eggplant, fish sauce caramel, thai basil	
Octopus, lettuce cup, sweet chili sauce, pickled fennel	
Head on shrimp, yuzu kosho vinaigrette, black garlic	12
Avocado, grapefruit, watercress, sweet sesame dressing	12
Beef tongue, pickled mustard and caraway seed, kimchi aioli	12
Confit of Quail, five spice molasses glaze, plum sauce, mandarin pancake	12
Pork belly	12

BAR + REFUGE

PLY

PLY is a new bar, restaurant and creative space based on Stevenson Square, the creative heart of the city. Apart from being home to a doodle wall and book exchange, PLY hosts regular exhibitions by international artists. Instruct Studio was tasked with creating a cohesive visual style across interior, print and digital. The involvement from the very beginning of the project allowed them to be rid of preconceptions, and to explore and experiment with themes relating to the materials found within the site.

Studio: Instruct Studio
Designer: John Owens, Laura Jackson, Ellie Thomas
Photographer: Sebastian Matthes

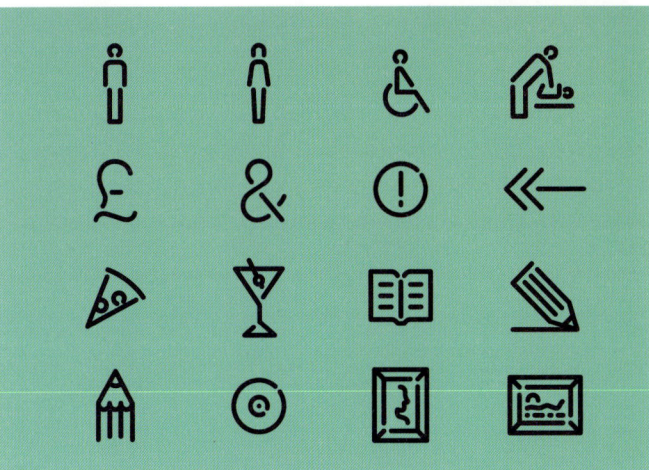

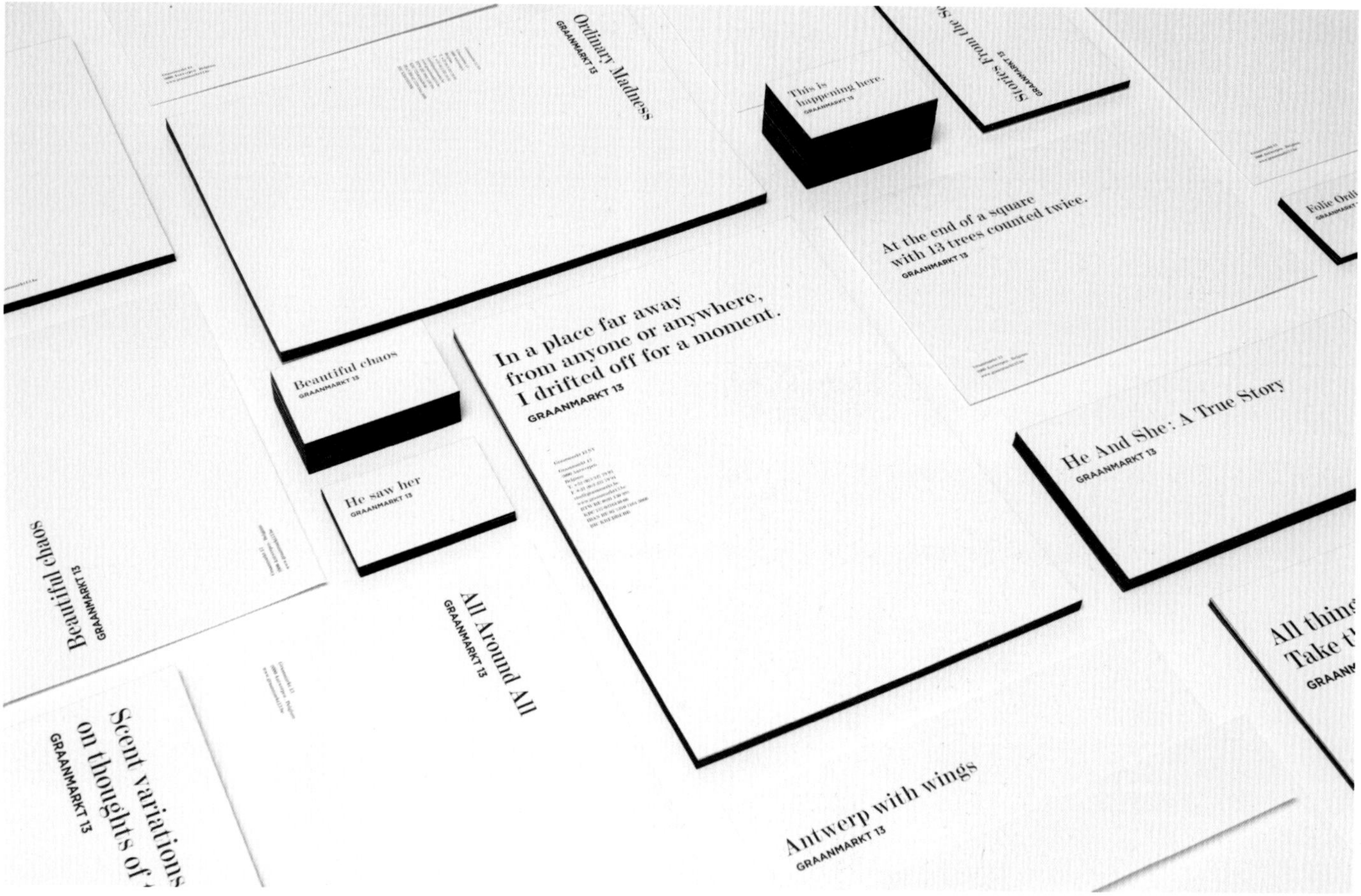

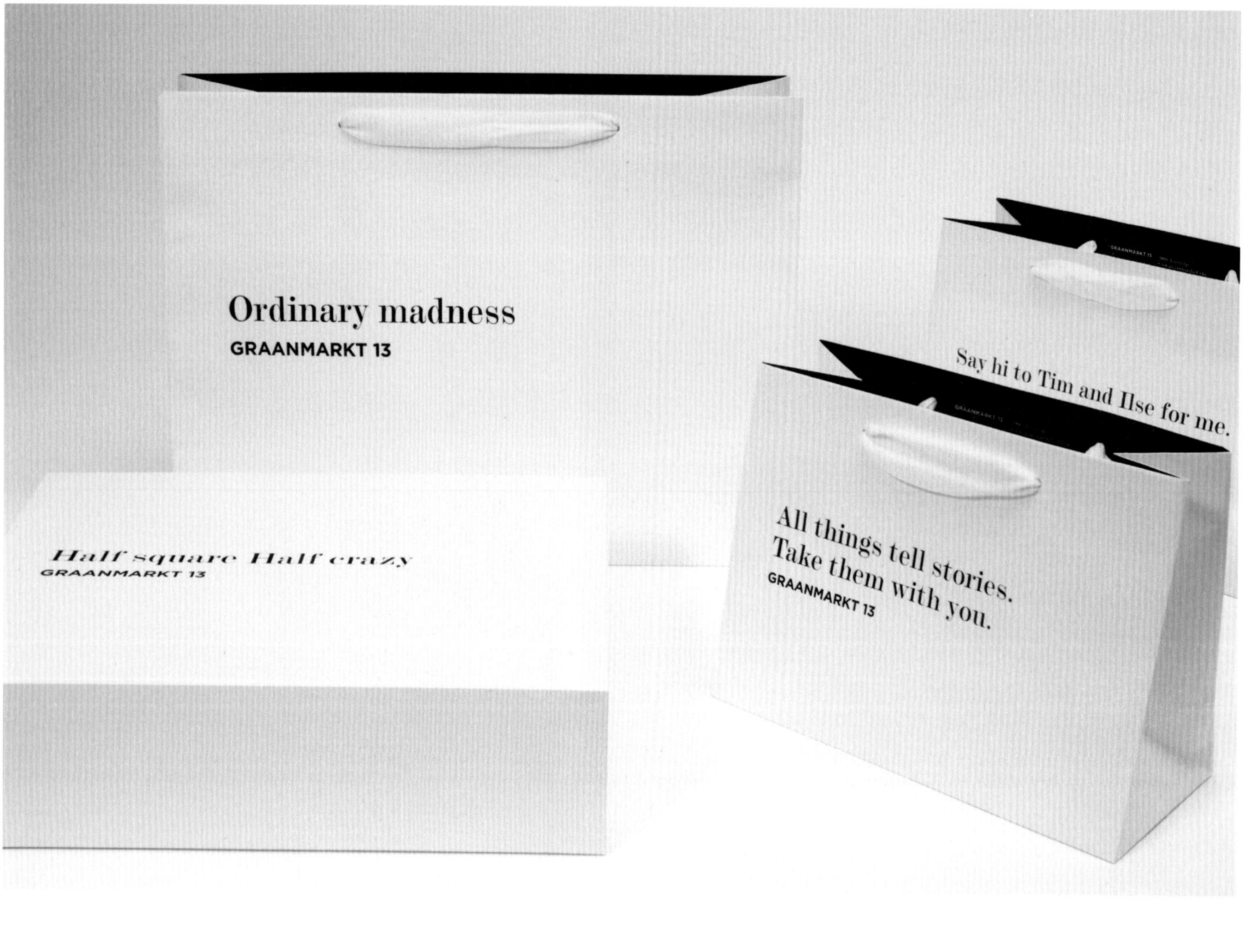

Graanmarkt 13

Graanmarkt 13 is a restaurant, a concept store, a gallery and an apartment all under one roof. Chef Seppe Nobels acquired a reputation for his sensational dishes prepared with local vegetables. The objective was to create a visual identity that presents this place as a destination with a story. The idea behind is anti-branding movement. Instead of a fixed logo, the identity employs a tone-of-voice and a story, with the address "Graanmarkt 13" as the one and only signature.

Studio: Base Design
Architect: Vincent Van Duysen
Scenographer: Bob Verhelst
Photographer: Base Design, Coffeeklatch, Frederik Vercruysse

Never Ending Story

Never Ending Story is a restaurant-cum-concept shop-cum-exhibition space based on a widely loved illustration book by Taiwanese illustrator Jimmy. The place offers different local dishes and art exhibitions in different seasons, allowing customers to experience the illustrator's every story. FMS aimed to create a versatile visual identity that complements the concept of never ending story by using 2D graphics to create 3D spaces. The graphics have adopted the often-seen elements in Jimmy's illustration book: the moon, the bird and the rabbit.

Studio: Five Metal Shop
Designer: Chou Yu Ling, Kuo Yi Chiau

NEVER ENDING STORY

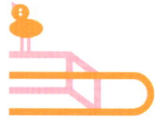  

 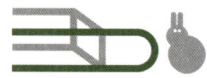

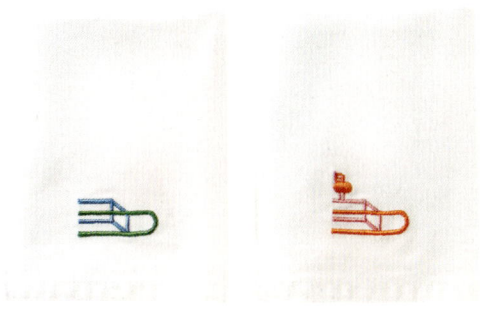

No.1, Sec.1, Bade Rd., Zhongzheng Dist., Taipei City, Taiwan

PART 2 /
Cafés and Bakeries

204—253

20 projects

Kuglóf

The hungarian word Kuglóf means bundt cake, which has been a very popular dessert baked in a metal pan since the 19th century. The branding task was to articulate the aura of the café. The identity features clean and light illustrations of a couple enjoying their breakfast and dinner at Kuglóf. Consistently styled icons were created for the packaging of the creams and pastries.

Designer: Diana Ghyczy
Photographer: Dorka Meleg

Coffee House London

London is a city deeply rooted in its traditions, history and architecture. Loyalties are formed in childhood and honored for a lifetime. Accordingly, the branding is not just to show the outstanding benefits of the product but to weave these assets into the themes of London culture, combining the cultural heritage of coffee drinks with the distinctive, one-of-a-kind pleasures of London House coffees.

Studio: Reynolds and Reyner
Designer: Alexander Andreyev, Artyom Kulik

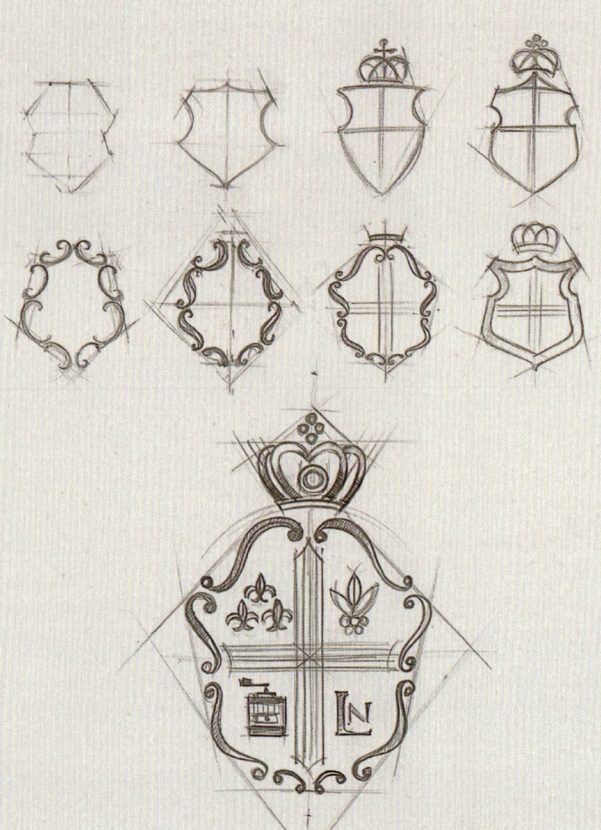

Cafe Decada

Cafe & Gallery Decada is located in Liben district in front of an abandoned railway track. In the identity design, the designer made use of motifs of coffee plant, historical photographs and graphic element of globe. The Globe is linked with the famous building Palace of World which used to be the biggest culture center of Liben. All graphics were manually screen printed on 1.5 mm recycled cardboard. The drink menu was hand tied with bookbinding tape and screws.

Studio: Lilkudley
Designer: Petr Kudláček

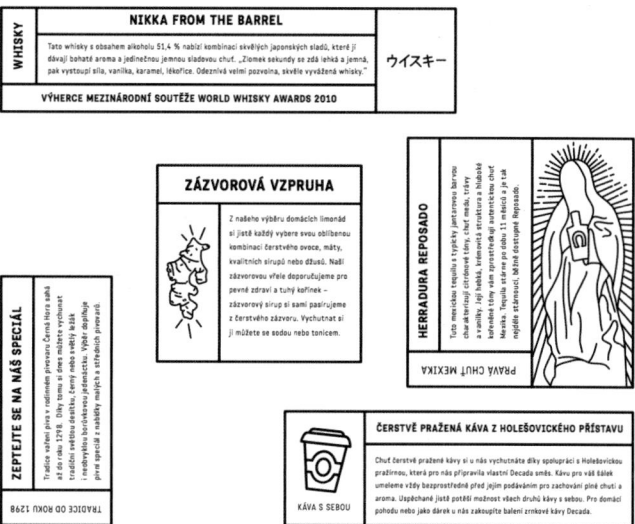

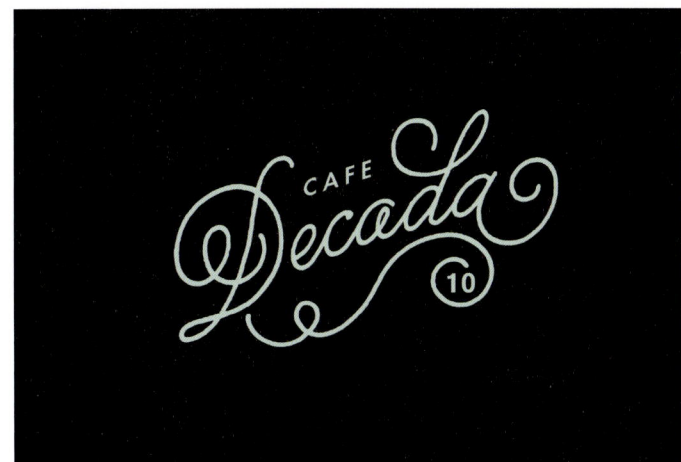

Vacínova 876/10, Prague, Czech Republic

Le Marché Cafe

Le Marché Cafe is a gourmet neighborhood café located in Miami, proudly serving carefully selected pastries and eats sourced locally and baked onsite. The assignment was to develop the brand identity, print collaterals and menu board. With a large variety of brand touchpoints ranging from digital to print to packaging applications, three variations of the logo were developed for maximum versatility.

Designer: Jiani Lu

1700 SW 2ND AVE, Miami, FL 33129, USA

Café Frida

Situated by the port, the coffee shop offers a view on the St-Lawrence River and a comfortable décor, along with coffee and beer, toasts and sweets. The hand-painted floral pattern in the branding was meant to pay tribute to the Mexican artist Frida Kahlo and her inspirational flower filled paintings.

Designer: Marie-Michelle Dupuis, Pier-Luc Cossette

Studio: Foreign Policy

Papa Palheta

This experience kit for Papa Palheta was designed to reflect the brand's combination of its strong coffee roots with the pursuit of sustainability. With consideration of the sensory elements, a recycled pulp paper card made with blended coffee chaff which is underused after coffee roasting, prompts the customers to repurpose it whether as a bookmark or thank-you card. To encourage the exploration of coffee culture, there are add-ons like a tasting notes sheet, an informative brewing guide and a cake recipe. In contrast with the earth tones, the color scheme of florescent orange and cobalt blue provides a pop of color, enlivening the common brown packaging of coffee.

150 Tyrwhitt Road, Singapore

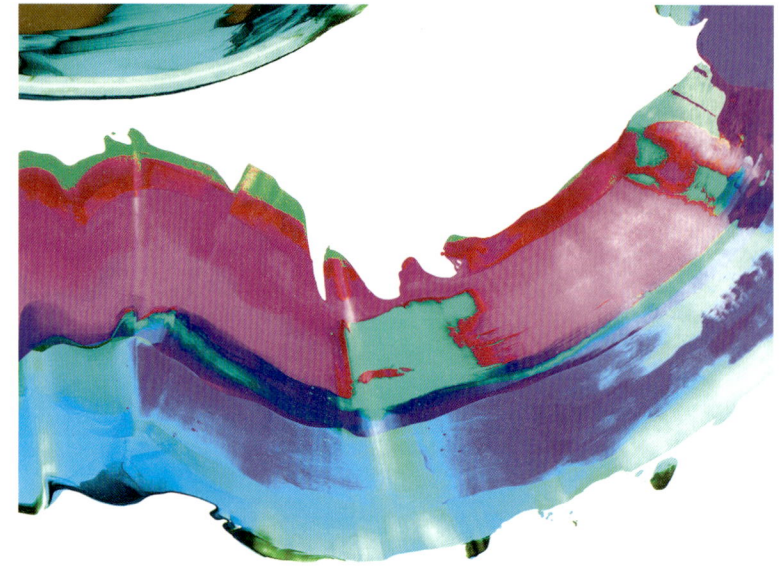

Coffee Maker

Coffee Maker is a cozy little coffee shop located in Arkhangelsk selling high quality coffee-to-go. A custom pattern was created as the basic element for the identity. Its bold color combination differentiates the café from the traditional ones, reflecting the owners' delightful characteristics.

Studio: Logomachine
Designer: Anton, Arina
Art Director: Regina

No. Six Depot

No. Six Depot is a family owned, small-batch coffee roaster and café nested in the beautiful Berkshires. Located in a historic train station on 6 Depot Street, they serve teas, salts and coffee from small farms and roast on location. The identity juxtaposes a mix of unique rural and modern elements, drawing inspiration from their backyard railroad and unique approach to keeping it simple and making it true.

Studio: Perky Bros
Designer: Jefferson Perky
Photographer: Jennifer May

Sei Kee Cafe

Since 1965, Sei Kee Cafe has made its name with its specialty clay pot brewed coffee and milk tea prepared in a family recipe. The café, now run by the third generation, opened its new concept takeout branch where customers could go on a journey back to the old time, accomplished by a nostalgic identity, hand painted logo and vintage interior.

Designer: Tun Ho

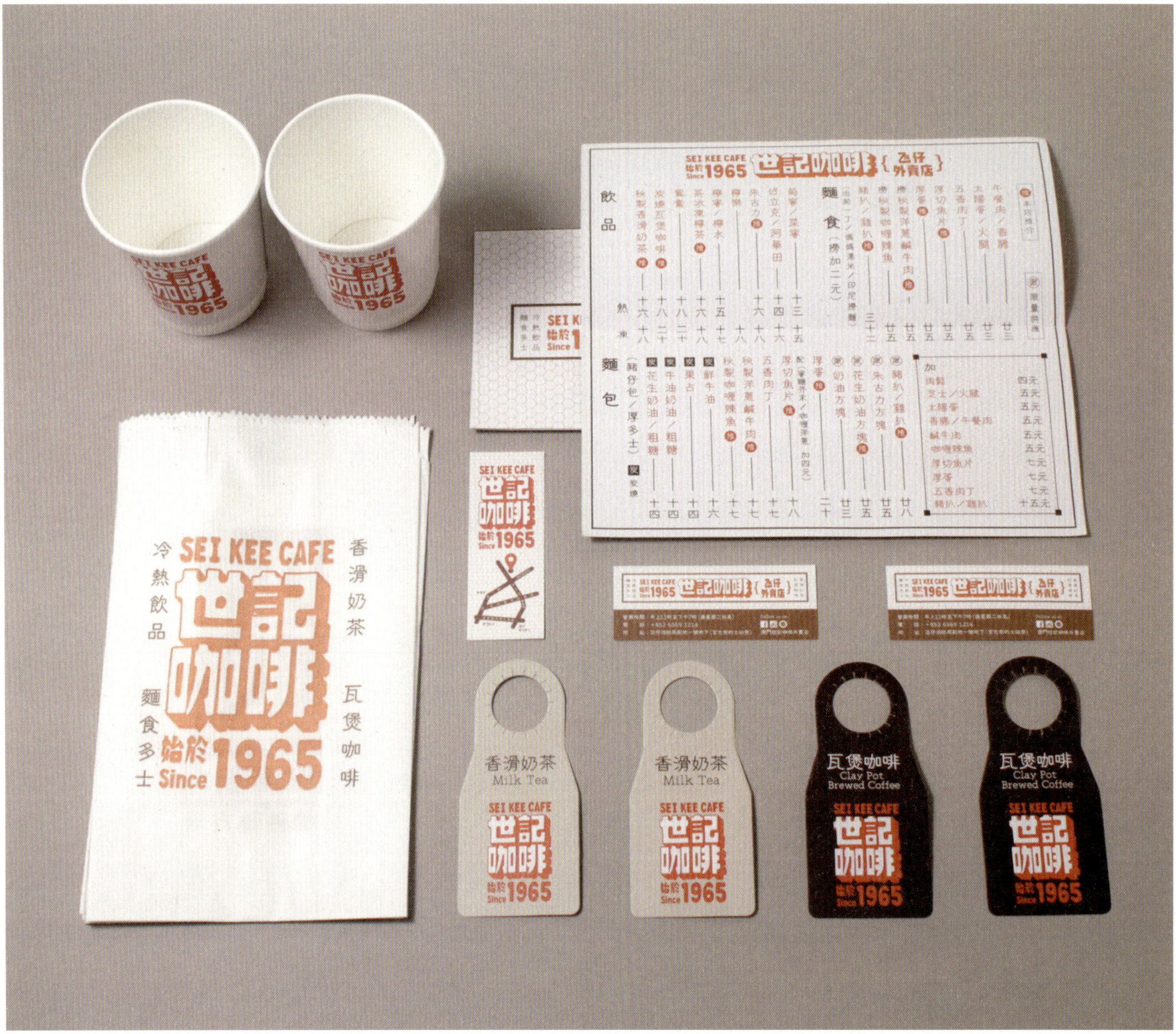

Largo dos Bombeiros, No 1, R/C, Taipa, Macau

Abarrotes Delirio

Abarrotes Delirio conveys a new gastronomical street culture through its authentic gourmet meals. The branding objective was to communicate the brand's concept of closeness and authenticity based on practicality, simplicity and the organic provenance of the ingredients. The contrast between the concepts of a corner shop and a gourmet one is resolved through a neutral and pristine design style.

Studio: Savvy
Interior: Habitación 116

Colima No. 114, Cuauhtémoc, Roma Nte., 06700 Ciudad de México, D.F, México

Galician Strudel

The residents in Kyiv love to visit the ancient city Lviv on holidays, go for a stroll in the old streets with smell of coffee and fresh bakery. This is how Galician strudel was established, being a small Lviv in Kyiv. And the branding was developed resembling a typical Lviv bakery. People in Lviv treat family values reverently and pass them from generation to generation, so families of bakers, craftsmen and artists could be found. The influential families always had their own abbreviations, seals and even ornaments, which became the important elements in this visual identity. Brown colors, craft paper and wax seals were used to highlight the vintage style.

Designer: Olena Fedorova
DTP: Maksym Finko

● 18 Saksaganskogo str., Kiev, Ukraine

The Dough Collective

The Dough Collective is a chain of premium Australian bakeries with an accessible price. The branding task was to bring elements of both old and new together to create a new image on a relatively small budget. While the look of the store took its roots from a more Asian concept, a strong western element was featured in the new design. Images of bread were used to create iconic patterns applied in the graphic design and floor tiles.

Studio: The Creative Method
Creative Director: Tony Ibbotson
Designer: Tim Heyer, Elina Lahti

Don de l'Amour

Don de l'Amour is a French Bakery specialized in home-baked desserts. The use of a warm pastel pink as the main color for the identity aims to convey freshness and sweetness. Enhanced by a custom hand drawn logotype, the branding is inviting and delicate at the same time, transmitting the core values of the bakery: delivering fresh and delicate treats every day.

Designer: Aurelie Maron

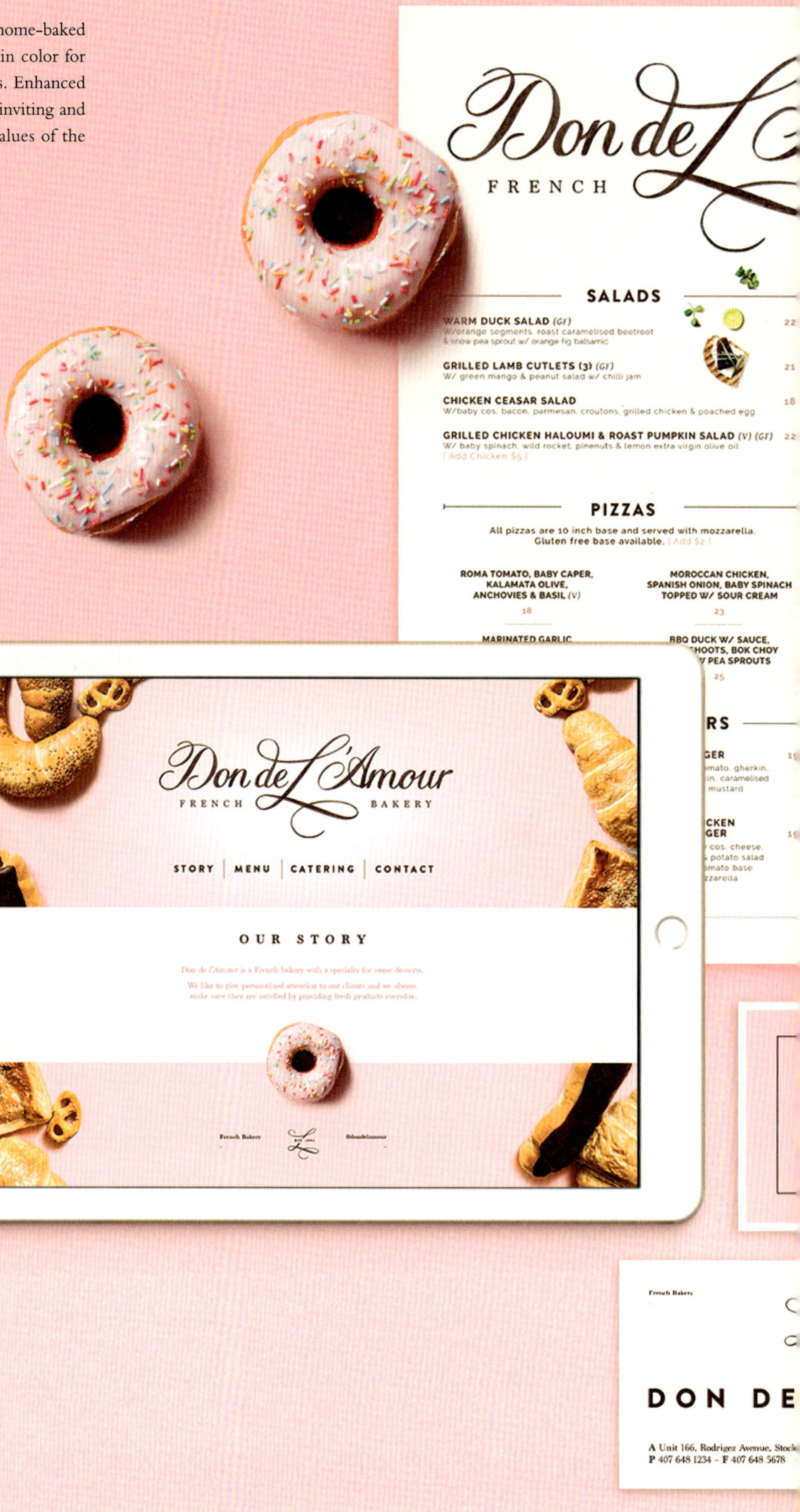

MAINS

TWICE ROAST PORK BELLY (GF) — 27
W/ sweet & sour cabbage & spiced roast apple

CRUMBED LAMB CUTLETS — 29
W/ roast sweet potato, baby spinach, rocket pesto & traditional gravy

FISH — 31
W/ bok choy, choy sum, shitake mushroom & chilli, coriander soy broth

BEEF & RED WINE PIE — 24
W/ mushy peas & mash

OSSO BUCCO — 26
W/ roast sweet potato & parnip, tomato compote

FAVOURITES

BATTERED FISH & CHIPS — 22
W/ egg & caper tartare & lemon wedges

CHICKEN SCHNITZEL, LIGHT SAGE & JAPANESE BREAD CRUMBED — 22
W/ coleslaw & chips served w/ garlic aoli

CHICKEN PARMINGANA — 24
W/ napoli sauce, mozzarella cheese, chips & rocket & parmasan salad

FISH OF THE DAY — MARKET PRICE

SPECIALS

All steaks served with mesclun salad
or vegetables & chips or mash.

ACCO 150 DAY SIRLION 300 GM GRAIN FED — 25

NOLANS PRIVATE SELECTION RIB EYE ON THE BONE 400 GM 150 DAY GRAIN FED — 35

RANGERS VALLEY SCOTCH FILLET 300 GM 300 GRAIN FED — 32

SURF & TURF, SIRLION STEAK 300GM, BBQ PRAWNS & BEARNAISE SAUCE (2) — 39

CHICKEN SUPREME 250 GRM MARINATED IN GARLIC, LEMON, ROSEMARY — 25

Choice Of Sauces: Mushroom, Pepper, Dianne, Traditional Gravy, Aoli, Pirri Pirri, Bearnaise | Extra Sauce $2 |

KIDS MEALS

GRILLED CHICKEN BURGER, LETTUCE & CHEESE W/ CHIPS

CRUMBED FISH BITES W/ CHIPS

ORRICHEE BEEF RAGOUT

CHICKEN & MUSHROOM RISOTTO

BEEF & CHEESE BURGER W/ CHIPS

$8

KIDS ICE CREAM ASSORTED FLAVOURS $4.50

SIDES

Coleslaw 4

Potato Salad w/ Gherkin, Bacon, Egg & Fresh Mayo 4

Creamy Mashed Potato 6

Steak Fries Bowl (w/ aoli) 9

Side 4

Seasoned Potato Weges 10

Onion Rings 7

Carlotta

Carlotta is a traditional Mexican style bakery where folkloric pastries such as conchas and buñuelos are prepared. The branding adopts graphic styles from El Porfiriato, a historical period in which Mexico was under the rule of President Porfirio Diaz, a man heavily influenced by French customs, art and architecture. Official documents from that era were used as main visual references to redesign these classic typographic styles. The embrace of delicacy and elegance are represented in the subtle arrangement of flowers as the main pattern. This element brings each part together with a black frame to settle the movement it creates, thus preserving the brand's personality.

Studio: Anagrama

Studio: MONOGRAM
Designer: Kris Mcknight

Maitre Choux

Maitre Choux is a modern version of a French patisserie that makes exceptional choux pastries, taking pride in having one of the finest pastry chefs in London. Drawing inspiration from the products themselves, the brand identity harnessed the simplicity and elegance of geometry to create an eye-catching pattern, which is both distinctive and original. The polka-dot pattern allowed the designer to introduce a number of colors in a sophisticated way to reflect the creativity and artistry of the product.

15 Harrington Road, London SW7 3ES, UK

Enjoyer

Enjoyer is an all-natural fruit bar and ice cream shop offering countless flavors of gelato, sorbet, juice and smoothie. The visual identity takes on the celebration of their thought about life that it should be lived to its full potential by having fun. The colorful confetti and the quirky logotype create a simple yet bold solution to express their cheerful attitude. The identity works mostly with black and white to highlight the vivid colors of the products.

Designer: Marton Borzak, Lili Koves
Interior Design: Inesa Malafej, Arunas Sukarevicius
Photographer: Daydream.com.sg

100 West Broadway, Glendale, CA 91210, USA

Sweet Spoon

Sweet Spoon is a frozen yogurt shop specialized in a variety of sweet products like cupcakes, cakepops, crepes, cronuts, etc. The aim was to generate an atmosphere close to a bakery and cupcake retail store, getting away from the typical aesthetics of a frozen yogurt shop such as saturated colors. The color pink was chosen to communicate the brand's image: sweet, fragile, delicious and feminine. Hand drawn logotype, chalkboard and homey interior add an even sweeter flavor to the shop.

Designer: Jimbo Bernaus

Remicone

The main logo depicts an imaginary production process of a soft serve ice-cream made out of a remicon truck. The typeface, interior and serving containers are designed to create a laboratory vibe. The initial R of Remicone, which is the symbol of the brand, is engraved on the door of the café. Each type of ice-cream served is illustrated as an icon on the menu so that the customers can easily make their orders.

Studio: YNL Design
Designer: Liz Yoona Lee
Interior: Betwin Space

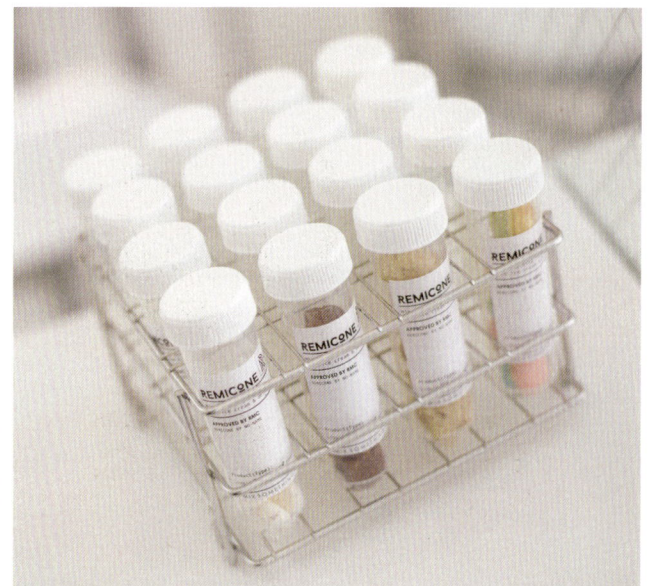
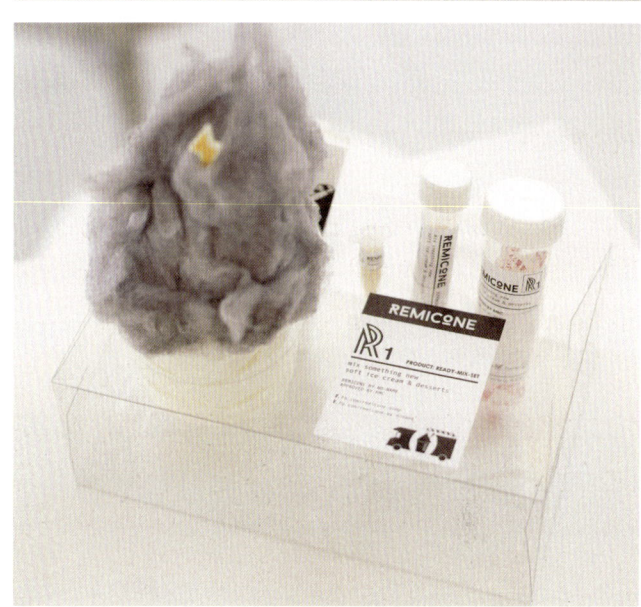

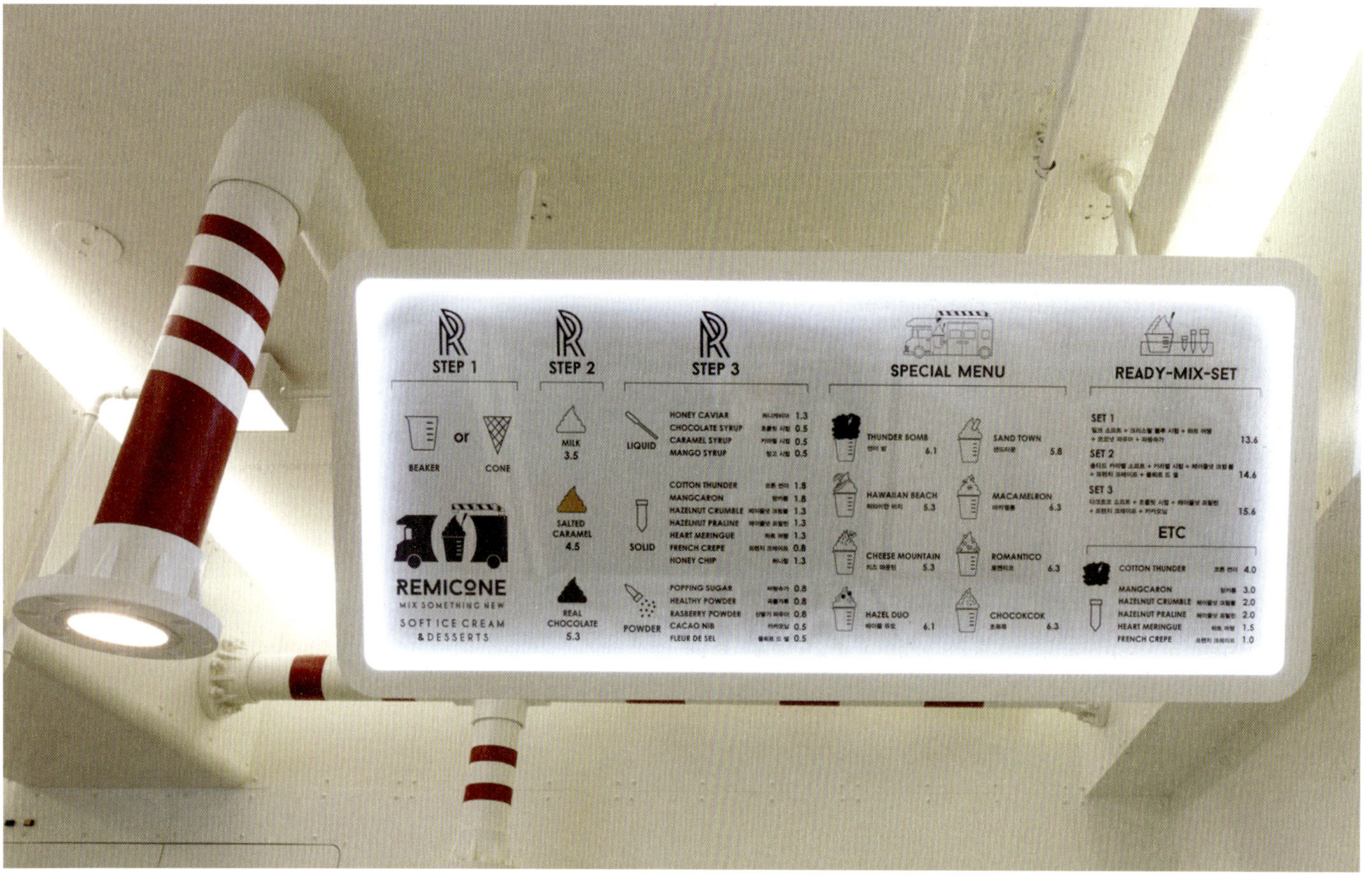

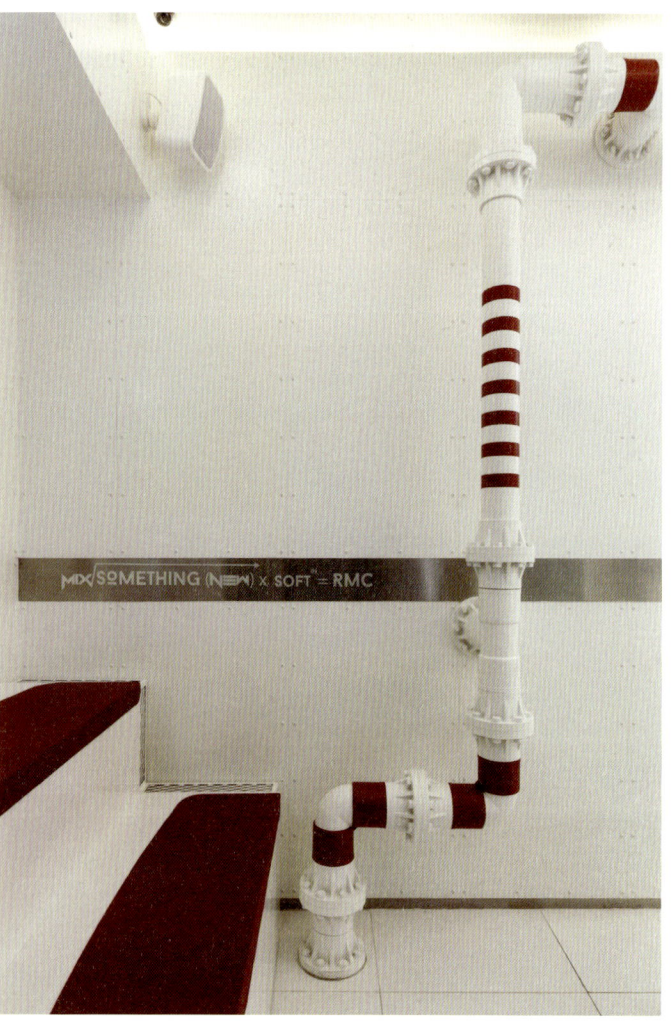

Cowch Dessert Bar

As Cowch's offer includes alcohol the brand image needed to be more mature but still light hearted and fun. The cow is featured as human in some scenarios to drive humor, warmth and a little attitude. Black and white or sepia tones were used to create a more sophisticated look but to also blend and contrast with the white interior. The cow is also cleverly integrated into a number of ideas such as the cocktail icon and the bottles stacked image on the wall.

Studio: The Creative Method
Creative Director: Tony Ibbotson
Designer: Tim Heyer

2/179 Grey St, South Brisbane QLD 4101, Australia

SAY HELLO TO MY LITTLE FRIENDS!

DESSERT COCKTAIL BAR

Casca

Casca is an artisan chocolate bar and café serving special flavored and spiced chocolate bonbons. The consistency and clarity of the graphic and interior design have given the brand a refreshing image. Apart from the basic structure of the interior, there are many noteworthy details such as the color blue that livens up the overall space, the lamp created from a porcelain teapot and cup.

Studio: kissmiklos
Photographer: Lackó Szögi

Jókai tér 3, Budapest, Hungary

INDEX

485 Design/James Showler
www.485design.co.nz
P146

A

Abraham Lule
www.behance.net/alule
P62

Adam&Co./Adam Larson
www.adamnco.com
P190

ADDA STUDIO
www.adda-studio.de
P26, 90

Anagrama
www.anagrama.com
P44, 236

Atelier Olschinsky
www.olschinsky.at
P188

Aurelie Maron
www.aureliemaron.com
P234

B

B3 Designers
www.b3designers.co.uk
P64

Base Design
www.basedesign.com
P198

Bond
www.bond-agency.com
P144

Brandon
www.brandon.ua
P120

Brownfox Studio
www.brownfoxstudio.com
P46

Bunker3022
www.bunker3022.com
P126

C

canaria inc.
www.canaria-world.com
P92

D

Diana Ghyczy
www.behance.net/eszkimo
P206

Dmitry Neal
www.dmitryneal.ru
P168

E

Enserio
www.enserio.ws
P20, 24

F

Farm Design
www.farmdesign.net
P108, 178

Five Metal Shop
www.fivemetalshop.com
P202

Foreign Policy
www.foreignpolicydesign.com
P36, 54, 68, 112, 218

Fork
www.madebyfork.ru
P128

FUTURA
www.byfutura.com
P86

G

Gabriel Finotti
www.gabrielfinotti.com
P172

G-sign
www.gsignlab.com
P152

H

Hongchang Shi, Biao Xiong
www.sunsund.com
P78

I

Instruct Studio
www.instructstudio.com
P194

Is Creative Studio
www.iscreativestudio.com
P150

J

Jerome & Zimmerman
www.jnz.mx
P156

Jiani Lu
www.lujiani.com
P212

Jimbo Bernaus
www.behance.net/JimboBernaus
P242

K

KIDSTUDIO
www.kidstudio.it
P52

KIND
www.kindnorway.com
P176

kissmiklos
www.kissmiklos.com
P94, 142, 252

Korolos Ibrahim
www.korolos.com
P10

 L

La Tortillería
www.latortilleria.com
P166

Le Maritime Studio
www.lemaritimestudio.com
P50

Lilkudley/Petr Kudláček
www.lilkudley.cz
P210

Logomachine
www.logomachine.net
P220

 M

Marie-Michelle Dupuis,
Pier-Luc Cossette
www.mariemd.work
www.plcossette.com
P216

Marton Borzak, Lili Koves
www.martonborzak.com
P240

Masquespacio
www.masquespacio.com
P32

Mast
www.manuelastorga.com
P136

Mind Design
www.minddesign.co.uk
P66

MONOGRAM/Kris Mcknight
www.monogramlondon.com
P238

MONOTYPO Studio
www.monotypo.com
P118, 132

 N

nendo
www.nendo.jp
P82

 O

Olena Fedorova
www.behance.net/olenafedorova
P230

ONE & ONE DESIGN/Li Wen
www.behance.net/1and1design
P104

ONO CREATES
www.onocreates.com
P100

 P

Pentagram
www.pentagram.com
P98

Perky Bros/Jefferson Perky
www.perkybros.com
P222

PLASMA NODO
www.plasmanodo.com
P40, 164

Pocket/Nicklas Lindholm Haslestad
www.nicklashaslestad.com
www.pocketoslo.com
P14

Province design
www.provincestudio.ru
P56

 R

Reynolds and Reyner
www.reynoldsandreyner.com
P208

S

Sarah Le Donne
www.sarahledonne.com
P48

Savvy
www.savvy-studio.net
P60, 182, 226

Substance
www.aworkofsubstance.com
P70, 114, 138, 160

T

The Creative Method
www.thecreativemethod.com
P58, 74, 232, 248

Tun Ho
www.behance.net/tunho
P224

U

Under
www.understhlm.se
P30

United Design Practice
www.uniteddesignpractice.com
P186

W

White Studio
www.whitestudio.pt
P18

Y

YNL Design
www.ynldesign.com
P244

ACKNOWLEDGEMENTS

We would like to thank all the designers and contributors who have been involved in the production of this book; their contributions have been indispensable to its creation. We would also like to express our gratitude to all the producers for their invaluable opinions and assistance throughout this project. And to the many others whose names are not credited but have made specific input in this book, we thank you for your continuous support.

FUTURE COOPERATIONS: If you wish to participate in SendPoints' future projects and publications, please send your website or portfolio to editor01@sendpoints.cn